Sagebrush Soldier

The "sagebrush soldier," or "one off [sic] the boys, 1876," as William Earl Smith wrote on the back of this portrait. Credit: Charles Watts

Sagebrush Soldier

*Private William Earl Smith's
View of the Sioux War of 1876*

by
Sherry L. Smith

University of Oklahoma Press : Norman

Library of Congress Cataloging-in-Publication Data

Smith, Sherry Lynn.
    Sagebrush soldier : Private William Earl Smith's view of the Sioux
War of 1876 / Sherry L. Smith.
        p. cm.
    Bibliography: p.
    ISBN 0-8061-2209-9 (cloth)
    ISBN 0-8061-3335-X (paper)
        1. Smith, William Earl, 1853?–1909. 2. Dakota Indians—Wars,
1876—Personal narratives. 3. Indians of North America—Powder
River Valley (Wyo. and Mont.)—Wars—Personal narratives. 4. United
States. Army. Cavalry, 4th—Biography. I. Smith, William Earl, 1853?–
1909. II. Title.
    E83.876.S65S65   1989
    973.8'2'0924—dc19   89-5408
                                                                           CIP

The sketches ornamenting the book are by Elizabeth L. Rosenberg, Cheyenne, Wyoming.

The paper in this book meets the guidelines for permanence and durability of the Committee on Production Guidelines for Book Longevity of the Council on Library Resources, Inc. ∞

2 3 4 5 6 7 8 9 10

For Bonnie
and All of Earl's Descendants

Contents

Illustrations

Maps

Preface

On a late November day in 1876, a soldier with the Fourth United States Cavalry pulled duty as pallbearer. Five men killed in a recent battle with the Northern Cheyennes awaited burial. As he gazed at the desolate winter scene before him—somewhere along the Bozeman Trail in Wyoming's Powder River Basin—he thought: "it was the hardest looking funeral I was ever at. . . . I would never like to be left in the ground in this wild cuntry whear no white man would ever see the place again."[1] One hundred and four years later I came very near that place while working for the Wyoming State Historic Preservation Office, for I was a historian searching for remnants of the famous Bozeman Trail. What I did not realize at the time was that I was following the path my great-grandfather, William Earl Smith, trod—that sagebrush soldier who, so many years before, served as pallbearer for the enlisted men killed in the Dull Knife battle. This was the same man who imagined no white person, let alone his own great-granddaughter, would pass that way again.

Only gradually was my personal connection with the place and these events made clear to me. Through my Bozeman Trail research, I discovered that my great-grandfather's regiment partici-

---

1. December 1, 1876. William Earl Smith diary, xerox copy and typescript in author's possession. The Newberry Library, Chicago, holds the original diary.

pated in the Powder River Expedition of autumn, 1876. Through
the generosity of family members who shared the soldier's precious diary with me, I learned something about the man. The
remarkable coincidence of my work in Wyoming and his—so
different in nature and yet so related—was exciting enough.
Moreover, the vitality, the charm, and the human appeal of his
1876 diary far exceeded my hopes.

The following year, with some concern about indulging myself
at the expense of students, I read portions of the diary to my
Indian-history class at the University of Colorado as part of a
lecture on the aftermath of the Little Bighorn Battle. Before long,
I realized my fears were unfounded. This was a document that
engaged students. William Earl Smith had something to say, not
only to his own descendants, but to the descendants of strangers
as well. At that point I decided, with the permission of the diary's
owner, to put it in print and share it with others.

Many histories of the Indian Wars line library bookshelves.
Among them, officers' accounts are certainly plentiful. The enlisted man's view, however, is far rarer, for most frontier soldiers
were either illiterate or not inclined to keep journals.[2] The diaries
of those who did write remain largely in the hands of descendants
who, perhaps, presume no one except family would find them
interesting. The value of Smith's view lies precisely in his obscu-
rity. He speaks only for himself, yet in some respects he certainly
speaks for many other frontier army soldiers. His preoccupation
with day-to-day comforts, with his own survival, and with his
nemesis, Sergeant Major Walsh, whom he describes as "a grate
big overgrown Irishman" strike the reader as endearingly mortal.
Smith's account reveals much about the common man's perception—and in some cases, lack of perception—of the military conquest of American Indians, the workings of an awesome, yet frequently blundering, nineteenth-century military force, and the
confounding, terrifying confusion of the bloodletting that accompanied the nation's westward expansion.

2. For a list of unpublished and published enlisted men's diaries, see Don
Rickey, Jr., *Forty Miles a Day on Beans and Hay*, 354–69; William E. Unrau,
ed., *Tending the Talking Wire: A Buck Soldier's View of the Indian Country:
1863–1866*, 7; and Edward M. Coffman, *The Old Army: A Portrait of the American Army in Peacetime, 1784–1898*, 497.

Further, this former railroad brakeman from Peoria, Illinois, has something to say not only about one of the West's little wars, but about other wars and the often-forgotten men who fought them. In *The Face of Battle*, John Keegan argues that "'Allowing combatants to speak for themselves' is not merely a permissible, but when and where possible, an essential ingredient of battle narrative and battle analysis."[3] This allows the historian to understand battle as it actually was, for it addresses how all participants felt about their predicament. Too often traditional military histories focus on the outcome of battle and ignore the events and character of the fighting itself. This approach necessarily eliminates the common soldier's perspective because he was not as concerned with the final outcome of the battle as was his general. The soldier's view, Keegan continues, "will be a much simpler one: it will centre on the issue of personal survival, to which the commander's 'win/loss' system of values may be, indeed often proves, irrelevant or directly hostile."[4] More is known about generals than about ordinary soldiers. Earl Smith's diary provides insight into why and how a common man fights.

Much of Smith's diary, however, addresses events other than those of the actual battle. Here one is struck by his illuminating comments about the relationships among enlisted men, noncommissioned officers, and commissioned officers—relationships characterized at times by affection, at others by brutality. The army caste system is vividly revealed in Smith's description of the expedition's daily life. He is acutely aware of a system that allows officers to abuse soldiers verbally and physically with few restraints. His resentment smolders just below the surface. His outrage ignites in Smith a sense of solidarity with other enlisted men. Perhaps more important for historical accuracy, Smith's account (as well as those of his military superiors) undermines the notion of a purposeful, stately, tightly organized campaign. Uncertainty, even chaos, marked some aspects of the expedition. His firsthand, day-to-day account brings out moments of apparent aimlessness and confusion. Alcohol, hardship, even boredom all play their parts in this story.

3. John Keegan, *The Face of Battle*, 32, 35.
4. Ibid., 47.

At the same time, it is important to remember that the Powder River Expedition was more than a United States Army or an Anglo-American experience. It was a complex, multicultural many-sided affair. Historian Patricia Limerick maintains that "the history of the West is a study of a place undergoing conquest."[5] Moreover, the West itself is an "important meeting ground, the point where Indian America, Latin America, Anglo-America, Afro-America, and Asia intersected" and the "workings of conquest tied these diverse groups into the same story."[6] Representatives of several of these groups certainly belong in any account of the Powder River Expedition. Rather than simply pitting Indian against white, this campaign found Shoshone, Pawnee, Sioux, and Southern Cheyenne people joining forces with the army against the Northern Cheyenne and Sioux who remained away from their agencies. Consequently, this story is a part of Indian history as much as military history. Indian history is so complex, Limerick cautions, that "historians have to be adept at putting together diverse versions of the same events."[7] This means juggling the tremendous diversity of Indian cultures, the conflicts both between and within tribes, and, in this account, the perspectives of Anglo-American soldiers, scouts, and officers.

In this book Private Smith's perspective serves as the focal point around which those of other participants' have been placed in an attempt to tell a story more complete than any single participant could offer, to demonstrate the complexity of a brief chapter in the annals of the Indian Wars, and to suggest multilayers of experience in what is often simplistically viewed as a two-sided event. For too long military historians have focused only on military perspectives and Indian historians on Indian perspectives.[8] This account attempts to bring these perspectives together, pro-

5. Patricia Nelson Limerick, *The Legacy of Conquest: The Unspoken Past of the American West*, 26.

6. Ibid., 26–27.

7. Ibid., 214.

8. For examples of both kinds of history, see Robert M. Utley, *Frontier Regulars: The U.S. Army and the Indian, 1866–1898*, and Peter Powell, *People of the Sacred Mountain: A History of the Northern Cheyenne Chiefs and Warrior Societies, 1838–1879*.

viding a more comprehensive view of events. The point here is to
juxtapose the military and the Northern Cheyenne, the officer and
the enlisted man, the Indian "ally" and the Indian "enemy," to
emphasize that a truly balanced history must include spokesmen
from all groups.

This, then, is William Earl Smith's story. But it is more. His
view is perhaps inevitably limited to insights into the enlisted
man's lot on the Powder River Expedition. He provides little information on other participants, particularly Indians. To under-
score this point, to enrich and balance the story, I quote other
diarists and letter writers who were in the same place at the same
time—using personal journals of several officers, one white scout,
and one noncommissioned officer, as well as the expedition's official correspondence.[9] Indian scouts' and auxiliaries' perspectives
come, unfortunately only indirectly, through an Anglo-American
who recorded their speeches at councils and a half-blood interpreter who reminisced about the campaign many years later. The
Northern Cheyennes' points of view, as well, stem mostly from
remembrances put to paper decades after the event and from
works of twentieth-century anthropologists and historians. Finally, I occasionally draw upon the works of participants who later
published accounts of this expedition.[10] The result is a work that

9. These include the unpublished diaries of Lt. Col. Richard Irving Dodge
and Lt. John Bourke and the published diaries of Luther North and Sgt. James
McClellan. For the McClellan diary, see Thomas R. Buecker, ed., "The Journals
of James S. McClellan, 1st. Sgt., Company H, 3rd Cavalry," *Annals of Wyoming*
57 (Spring 1985): 21–34.

10. Lt. Bourke attempted a record of Indian-scout statements in his journal.
William Garnett, interpreter for the Sioux on the expedition, reminisced about
the campaign in 1907 in an interview with Eli Seavey Ricker; notes are available
for researchers at the Nebraska State Historical Society, Lincoln. Accounts by
Northern Cheyennes include those of John Stands in Timber, Wooden Leg, and
Two Moon. Two Moon was a source for Grinnell's *The Fighting Cheyennes*, and
Wooden Leg's account can be found in Thomas Marquis, *Wooden Leg: A Warrior
Who Fought Custer*. George Grinnell, Thomas Marquis, Margot Liberty, and
Peter Powell have all published accounts that preserve Northern Cheyenne per-
spectives. See George Bird Grinnell, *The Fighting Cheyennes*; John Stands in
Timber and Margot Liberty, *Cheyenne Memories*; Thomas B. Marquis, *Wooden
Leg: A Warrior Who Fought Custer*; Peter J. Powell, *People of the Sacred Mountain:
A History of the Northern Cheyenne Chiefs and Warrior Societies, 1830–1879*, 2

departs from traditional edited books of primary sources.[11] Rather than present participants' accounts separately, this approach aims for greater integration of perspectives. It rests on the belief that such a method lends itself to a closer approximation of the truth.

A few words about Smith's diary as a historical document are in order. The original is handwritten, in diary fashion, with daily entries. The descriptions of physical landscapes, conversations, fleeting moments of anger or melancholy have an immediacy that could have come only from on-the-spot notation. Yet the document gives the appearance of having been copied—perhaps from another, smaller field journal—for Smith's account is presented on legal-sized sheets of paper, in ink, and in a neat hand. In addition, Smith occasionally speaks of future events. For example, in introducing a bunkmate, he indicates this man remained his "bunkie" through the following spring. Such asides give the journal an occasional retrospective air. A notation at the bottom of a poem celebrating the "Red Rock Canon Fight," indicates the poem was copied September 16, 1877, by Charles S. Fowler for Smith at Fort Wallace, Kansas. Quite possibly Fowler, or someone else with handwriting more legible than Smith's, copied the entire journal at this time. The document, nevertheless, retains the immediacy and point of view of a contemporary record rather than a reminiscence.

Of the document's authenticity I have no doubt. It was given to Earl Smith, grandson and namesake of the diarist, by Smith's widow. Further, the voice of the 1876 diary matches that of a small 1878 diary that clearly was a field journal. In the later diary,

---

vols.; and Powell, *Sweet Medicine: The Continuing Role of the Sacred Arrows, the Sun Dance, and the Sacred Buffalo Hat in Northern Cheyenne History*, vol. 1. Among the published accounts by white participants consulted here are John G. Bourke, *Mackenzie's Last Fight with the Cheyennes: A Winter Campaign in Wyoming and Montana*; Luther North, *Man of the Plains: Recollections of Luther North, 1856–1882*; and Homer W. Wheeler, *The Frontier Trail Or From Cowboy to Colonel*.

11. I have used J. S. Holliday, *The World Rushed In: The California Gold Rush Experience*, as a model. In this book, Holliday integrates William Swain's gold rush diary and his letters home with letters that Swain received from his wife and brother (who were back in New York) and accounts of other gold rushers. The result is a more nearly complete picture of the experience.

in which Smith used a pencil, the handwriting is difficult to deci-
pher. This may be the reason he copied, or had someone else
copy, his earlier work.

Typical of many nineteenth-century Americans, Smith spelled
erratically. Most often, if he were uncertain about a word, he
spelled it phonetically. Whenever possible I have left those spell-
ings uncorrected to convey the flavor and even the force of his
own voice. Occasionally, however, for purposes of clarity and
smooth reading I standardized a phonetic spelling. For the same
reasons, I added punctuation. Laced throughout Smith's narrative
the reader will find testimony from other participants of the Sioux
War of autumn and winter 1876. Here, too, I occasionally added
punctuation and paragraph construction.

In many ways the completion of this project was a family endeavor. Several individuals deserve special notice for their generosity and hard work. Charles Smith and the late Earl F. Smith,
along with Norene Berry, shared the original diaries with the rest
of the Smiths. Walter and Arlite Smith Marquardt and Carol
Ward carefully transcribed the 1876 and 1878 diaries from the
original manuscripts. The Marquardts, Audrey Smith Ward, and
my father, Atwood Earl Smith, conducted hours of research in
St. Louis, Missouri; Peoria, Illinois; Wrentham, Massachusetts;
Providence, Rhode Island; Salt Lake City, Utah; and Chicago,
Illinois, tracking down the particulars of Earl Smith's background
and that of his parents. My mother, Adeline Behnke Smith, and
my siblings, Bonnie Smith, Barbara SilverSmith, and Brian Smith
helped with research, read the manuscript, and offered valuable
editorial advice and encouragement. In addition, Charles Watts
and Charles Smith shared family photographs. We all owe a special debt of gratitude to Aunt Carrie Smith Watts, who loved the
family history and provided the initial information that led to this
book.

A number of others also contributed to this project. Michael
Pilgrim of the National Archives proved especially helpful in
ferreting out information on both officers and enlisted men
of the 1876 Powder River Expedition. Marie Capps, United
States Military Academy Library, and John Aubrey, Newberry
Library, located relevant papers as well. Patricia Nelson Limerick,

Thomas R. Buecker, Margot Liberty, Paul Hedren, and William Leckie read earlier versions of this work and offered valuable suggestions for improvement. Tom Buecker also shared typescripts of Sergeant James S. McClellan's diaries with me. Sheila Bricher-Wade and Eileen Starr, of the Wyoming State Historic Preservation Office, became special friends as well as valued professional collaborators as we searched for the Bozeman Trail and tried to preserve remnants of it. Norris, Ken, and Cheri Graves were gracious enough to allow me several visits to the battlefield, which now is a part of their ranch. A Wyoming Council for the Humanities Fellowship for Independent Study and Research made possible a research trip to the National Archives. Finally, my husband and most valued friend, Robert W. Righter, read several versions of this work, offered editorial advice and unstinting encouragement, and—most generous of all—listened.

Sagebrush Soldier

Chapter 1

Background

It was nearly dawn, November 25, 1876. William Earl Smith waited for Colonel Ranald Mackenzie's order to charge the quiet Northern Cheyenne village set in a rimrocked valley of the Big Horn Mountains. As he tightened the girth on his horse's saddle, he later wrote in his journal, "It was now I thought of [the] Custer Masacree [sic] and began to think what I was about to go into."

Only a few years before Smith had worked as a railroad brakeman in Illinois. But fortune led to his enlistment in the army in 1876, and the forces of history led to this dramatic moment—a crucial one for the Northern Cheyennes, who were determined to maintain their possession of the Powder River country, and for the United States policymakers, who were determined to end that possession.

Such issues did not trouble Smith, however. In this respect he was no doubt typical of most of the enlisted men who sat poised to attack the Indian "enemy." In fact, from all appearances there was little to distinguish this soldier from hundreds of others. He was of average build and average height. He had dark brown hair and blue eyes, and he sported the same winter campaign garments issued to the other recruits. But Private Smith was different in at least one respect: he kept a diary of this Powder River Expedition and of the attack on the village of Morning Star (or Dull Knife, as he was better known to whites). Moreover, for a time, he served as orderly to Ranald Mackenzie—a position offering an extraordinary opportunity to contrast the lot of officers with that of enlisted men, to overhear officers' conversations, and to observe some of the frontier army's most famous commanders in both battle and bottle.

Private William Earl Smith's origins are somewhat obscure. Earl, as he was known to his family, was born around 1853 in Peoria, Illinois. The identity of his biological parents is uncertain, but sometime during the 1850s an innkeeper named William Smith adopted him. Smith's wife, Jane Elizabeth Foster, may have been the boy's mother. William Smith had moved to Peoria in 1849 from St. Louis to lease the Peoria House, and he remained its proprietor until 1855. At that point, this midwestern entrepreneur retired from the hotel business to engage in real estate and, under the name of William Smith and Company, to manufacture alcohol, camphene, and pure spirits. Until his death in 1859, at age forty-nine, the Rhode Island–born Smith had provided his family (which by then included two more children—a daughter, Jennie, and a son, Charles) with a comfortable middle class life.[1]

Nineteen years younger than her husband, Jane Foster was the daughter of a New England sea captain, Benjamin F. Foster, who mastered ships from Rhode Island to Massachusetts and even New Orleans, and Zeolide Brown Foster of Wrentham, Massachusetts. The Fosters moved to St. Louis sometime in the 1840s. In 1847 the Reverend W. H. Eliot, a well-known St. Louis Unitarian minister, married Jane to a man named Henry Green Smith in that city. But by 1850 she was living in the Peoria House, along

---

1. Most of the information about William Smith is derived from his obituary, which appeared in the *Peoria Transcript*, Aug. 31, 1859. Other sources of information include Peoria City directories for the 1850s and the 1850 federal census. See "1850–Illinois–Peoria Co.–Peoria" census, microfilm copy, Newberry Library, 905.942. According to a WPA "History of Peoria," the Peoria House originally opened as the Planters Hotel in 1840. It was 3 stories tall and had 37 sleeping rooms. Col. A. O. Garrett, who built it, sold the property to William Smith and his partner, Asabel Hurlburt, in 1849. They changed the name to Peoria House. In 1854, Smith sold his interest to Mr. Warren Hall. The Peoria House served as headquarters for both Abraham Lincoln and Stephen A. Douglas during their visits to Peoria. See "History of Peoria," WPA File, Bradley University, Peoria, Illinois.

with her widowed mother and William Smith, where all apparently prospered.[2]

It is difficult to say when William and Jane married, because no record of the wedding can be found in either St. Louis or Peoria. It is possible that Henry and William Smith were brothers and that after Henry's death Jane married William. Jane would later claim that Earl was susceptible to cholera—perhaps a clue to Henry's demise in the cholera epidemics so common at midcentury. At any rate, by 1855, Jane and William were married and producing their own offspring. By the time of his death in 1859, William had adopted Earl.[3]

Eleven months after William's death, Jane's mother died in Peoria. Several years later, her only sibling, Benjamin T. Foster, succumbed while serving as adjutant in the 108th Illinois Regiment of Volunteers.[4] Inheritances from her mother and husband no doubt relieved some of the young woman's anxieties, but she faced both relentless litigation from her husband's creditors and the challenge of raising three small children, ages eleven to four, by herself. Several star-crossed marriages increased Jane's financial and emotional turmoil. Her third husband was a potter from Vermont named Christopher Fenton. By 1866 she was married a fourth time, to Marshall Manley, a laborer.[5]

The latter partnership was far from harmonious, if divorce records are any window into the private lives of this nineteenth-century family. Unfortunately, Jane Manley failed to appear at the 1875 divorce proceedings and her side of the story remains unre-

2. *St. Louis Reveille,* Dec. 11, 1847; see also "1850 Illinois–Peoria Co.–Peoria," Newberry Library, 905.942.

3. In the copy of his will deposited at the Peoria County Courthouse, William Smith refers to Earl as his adopted son.

4. Jane Foster Smith's mother, Zeolide Foster, died on July 6, 1860, from consumption. Rev. W. H. Eliot, of St. Louis, preached the funeral sermon on July 8, in Peoria. See *Peoria Daily Transcript,* July 7, 1860; *Peoria Daily Democratic Union,* July 7 and 8, 1860. For information on Benjamin Foster, Jane Foster Smith's brother, see Benjamin T. Foster, Pension File No. WC42–257, RG 15, Records of the Veterans Administration, National Archives and Records Service (hereafter NARS).

5. See *Marshall D. Manley vs. Jane Manley, In Chancery For Divorce, Circuit Court, December Term, 1875,* Peoria County Courthouse, Peoria, Ill.

William Earl Smith, at age fourteen, in Peoria, Illinois, his home-
town. Credit: Charles Watts

corded. According to the estranged husband, the couple had lived together from 1866 until 1869, when Jane deserted his home and their son, George, "without any just or reasonable cause."[6] An 1870 census, however, indicates that the couple were still living together, along with George, Earl, Jennie, and Charles. Earl was identified as eighteen years old and a railroad brakeman. His mother, it was noted, maintained four thousand dollars in property apart from her husband.[7] Five years later, in the absence of Jane's testimony, the court granted Manley his divorce as well as custody of the child, George.[8]

After a presumably pleasant, even prosperous childhood, the death of his stepfather and his mother's marital and economic troubles undoubtedly colored Earl's adolescence. While his mother maintained some financial independence, he found it necessary to support himself, and by 1870 he was a railroadman. On Febru-

6. Ibid., 2.
7. See "1870–Illinois–Peoria Co.–Peoria" U.S. federal census, microfilm copy, Newberry Library, 51.
8. *Marshall D. Manley vs. Jane Manley*, 3.

ary 1, 1876, Smith marched into an army recruiting office in Chicago and agreed to a five-year enlistment. His reasons for joining the army are unknown. He left no record of these events. The Panic of 1873 had taken its toll on many lives, and perhaps Earl's was among them. According to one historian of the frontier army's enlisted men, a large number of recruits entered the service from the bottom rung of the economic ladder or after falling from an intermediate one. For them (and Earl may represent the latter) enlistment provided an alternative to unemployment and better pay than some unskilled jobs. Other recruits joined to escape boredom, find adventure, and see the West. For many young men, however, enlistment was a last resort. Civilian attitudes toward army regulars in post–Civil War America were not particularly favorable. In fact, suspicion of the military had characterized American views of the army for many years.[9] Certainly it was not a life of easy duty, fine food, generous pay, and cultured companionship. Recruits were not necessarily desperate, but a good number probably came close.

Whatever his reasons for enlisting, Private Smith passed a physical examination at the Chicago recruiting office—taking the first step that would lead him to his share of peril and hardship. He reported in at five feet, five inches, swore an oath of office at a nearby regimental station, received ill-fitting recruit clothing, and was sent to St. Louis Barracks, Missouri, for a minimum of training. After little more than one month's introduction to the austere, rigid system that was the regular army, including terrible food and harsh discipline, Private Smith was assigned to Company E, Fourth United States Cavalry on March 19. Nine days later he reported to his company at Fort Elliott, Texas, along with twelve other brand-new recruits, making a company of forty-six privates and fifty-four serviceable horses.[10]

9. Rickey, Jr., *Forty Miles*, 17–26; and Coffman, *Old Army*, 329–31, 334–35. Smith's mother later indicated she was unaware of his decision to enlist. Mrs. William Thompson to Mr. Henderson, Nov. 18, 1877, Box 2178, RG 94, Records of the Adjutant General's Office, Enlisted Branch, Letters Received, NARS.

10. See "Register of Enlistments on the U.S. Army, 1798–1914," M-233, Roll 4, 76:194, NARS; Enlistment Paper #101, Box 2032, RG 94, Records of the Adjutant General's Office, 1780s-1917, NARS; and Co. E, 4th U.S. Cavalry

We can only guess at Smith's reactions to his new life, but perusal of the muster rolls from the time of his arrival among the Fourth Cavalry and the beginning of his own account indicates at least one scrape with rigid army discipline in which he was fined ten dollars of his pay. For soldiers earning a base pay of thirteen dollars per month, this constituted a hefty penalty.[11] In addition to adjusting to army discipline, Smith had to adjust to army society. The gulf between commissioned officers and the rest of the troopers, noncommissioned officers and privates alike, was especially great, for the frontier army operated within a caste system of sorts, based on European models. Privates virtually were required to get permission from their first sergeant to speak to a commissioned officer, and personal interaction between private and officer rarely occurred, although this could change in the context of battle. This caste system did not sit well with many men, and an officer who considered himself innately superior to his soldiers would quickly earn their disrespect, even their enmity. But if an officer demonstrated military competency and treated the ranks like human beings, he could easily win their respect and even their affection.[12] The Fourth Cavalry's Colonel Ranald Mackenzie fell into the latter mold, and Private Smith soon developed respect and affection for his commander.

Ranald Mackenzie's boyhood, spent on farms along the Hudson River in New York and in Morristown, New Jersey, was more privileged and presumably more secure economically than Smith's. In autumn 1855, Ranald enrolled at Williams College. At the end of his junior year Mackenzie, who was the son of a naval officer, received an appointment to the United States Military

Muster Roll, Feb. 29, 1876–April 30, 1876, Box 968, RG 94, Records of the Adjutant General's Office, NARS. According to Don Rickey, Jr., after 1866 the U.S. Cavalry was authorized to include 64 privates per company. After the disaster at the Little Bighorn, the number was increased to 100, although the actual strength of cavalry companies was usually much lower. Rickey, *Forty Miles*, 48–49; Coffman, *Old Army*, 332–33, 336–38.

11. Co. E. 4th, U.S. Cavalry Muster Roll, April 30, 1876–June 30, 1876, Box 968, RG 94, Records of the Adjutant General's Office, NARS; Rickey, *Forty Miles*, 22; Coffman, *Old Army*, 346–50, 375–77.

12. Rickey, *Forty Miles*, 63, 67; Coffman, *Old Army*, 344–45.

Academy at West Point.[13] Washington Gladden, a classmate at Williams, later remembered his friend as: "very quiet, modest to shyness, and with a little lisp, Ranald was a good fellow; we all loved him and were both sorry and proud when the appointment [to West Point] came to him."[14] And so Private Smith's "Genrall" Mackenzie, looking not unlike the young Ralph Waldo Emerson, began his career with the army.

That career, of course, included an active role in the Civil War. At the close of that conflict, General Ulysses Grant pronounced Ranald Mackenzie the "most promising young officer in the Army."[15] Mackenzie had been wounded at the Second Battle of Bull Run and again at Petersburg. The latter injury, in fact, cost him two fingers on his right hand—a disability that later caught the attention of Indians who branded him "Bad Hand" on its account. It was, however, not his wounds but his unflagging courage (some would say recklessness) under fire, his insistence on an exacting discipline within the ranks, and his perseverance in battle which so impressed Grant. When the war ended, Mackenzie had attained, at age twenty-four, the rank of Brigadier General of Volunteers with the brevet rank of brigadier general in the regular army. In further recognition of his talents, Mackenzie, who had graduated at the head of his West Point class only four years before, was appointed colonel in the Forty-first Infantry and stationed along the Rio Grande in 1866. By 1871 he had received command of the Fourth Cavalry, and before long Philip Sheridan deemed Mackenzie not only the finest field officer in the army but the best Indian fighter as well.[16]

Gaining a reputation as a no-nonsense commander with an eccentric temperament, yet a leader who was neither petty nor malicious, Mackenzie engaged in a series of expeditions against tribes of the southern plains. In the early 1870s he attacked, with

13. Edward S. Wallace, "General Ranald Slidell Mackenzie: Indian Fighting Cavalryman," *Southwestern Historical Quarterly* 56 (Jan. 1953): 379; J.'Nell L. Pate, "Ranald S. Mackenzie," in Paul Andrew Hutton, *Soldiers West: Biographies From the Military Frontier*, 177–92.

14. Quoted in Wallace, "General Ranald Slidell Mackenzie," 382.

15. Ulysses Grant, *Personal Memoirs of U.S. Grant* 2:451.

16. Paul Andrew Hutton, *Phil Sheridan and His Army*, 219–21.

Colonel Ranald Mackenzie commanded all cavalry regiments during the Powder River Expedition. This portait was taken during the Civil War. Credit: National Archives and Records Administration, negative 111-B-2735

varied success, Comanches, Lipans, Kickapoos (although he violated the international boundary with Mexico to do so), Kiowas, and Southern Cheyennes. During the Red River War of 1874–75, he proved especially successful in routing a large Indian village in Palo Duro Canyon. Although only three fighting men died among the Comanches, Kiowas, and Cheyennes occupying the village, he struck a devastating blow by burning several hundred lodges and their contents and by shooting more than one hundred Indian ponies. This tactic was one he would pursue again—against the Cheyennes of the northern Rockies.[17]

Private Smith would serve as orderly to this famous officer, but for a time during the expedition his immediate superior would be

17. Wallace, "General Ranald Slidell Mackenzie," 386–90; Hutton, *Phil Sheridan*, 254.

another man. If Smith admired Colonel Mackenzie, he felt only contempt for Sergeant Major Stephen Walsh. By autumn 1876, Walsh had served with the Fourth Cavalry for eleven years, having originally enlisted in the army in April 1865 in New York City. After his choice of a military life, the Irish-born Walsh's career had ebbed and flowed. In 1869 he made sergeant major, but in 1871 he was reduced to private. Four years later, his fortune took another upward turn when he was promoted to corporal and attached to the field staff of the Fourth Cavalry. In November he reached the rank of sergeant and on May 17, 1876, at age forty-three, Walsh was again promoted to sergeant major, the rank he held when Private Smith met him.[18]

Smith understood the power of a sergeant to make life miserable for the lowly private. Noncommissioned officers, far more than anything or anyone else, determined the everyday fates of privates such as Smith. According to historian Don Rickey, "If a single word were chosen to describe the noncommissioned officers of the Indian Wars army, that word would have to be—*tough*."[19] The administration of company affairs fell to the first sergeant, who in turn often passed it along to sergeants and corporals. In addition, commissioned officers frequently left informal punishment, which could be humiliating as well as illegal, to the sergeants. Just as privates came from all social, ethnic, and economic backgrounds, the same held true for noncommissioned officers.[20] The result was tremendous potential for resentment, conflict, and even violence between privates and their immediate superiors.

As Smith learned the ways of army society through the spring and summer of 1876, his regiment quietly attended to regular

18. Sgt. Maj. Stephan Walsh was born in Ireland in 1833. According to the enlistment register, he was 5 feet 8 and one-half inches tall, had dark hair and blue eyes. Before enlisting in the army, he was a clerk. See "Registers of Enlistments in the U.S. Army, 1798–1914," Microcopy M-233, Roll 30, NARS, 61:295. Information on Walsh's seesaw military career can be found in various muster rolls of the Fourth Cavalry. See, in particular, April 30–June 30, 1875; Oct. 31–Dec. 31, 1875; and April 30–June 30, 1876, Field Staff and Band Muster Rolls, Fourth U.S. Cavalry, Box 958, RG 94, Records of the Adjutant General's Office, NARS. See also Stephan Walsh's Pension File, #375129, RG 15, NARS.

19. Rickey, *Forty Miles*, 59.

20. Ibid., 60–63.

garrison and occasional escort duties in Texas. He had certainly heard of Lieutenant Colonel George Custer's fate on the Little Big-horn in June and perhaps even shared the sentiments of other soldiers who hoped to avenge Custer and his men's deaths before the year was out. By August, Smith, Walsh, and Mackenzie had arrived at Camp Robinson, Nebraska. Several months later, they would seek and gain such revenge.

Of the Sioux and their allies, the Northern Cheyennes, or of the issues that pitted army against Indian in Dakota territory, Smith probably knew nothing. Although the events of autumn 1876 would lead him to their country as part of a military force determined to compel their surrender, American troopers were not the first to dislodge the Cheyennes from their homes. They were a people long accustomed to pressure from others with whom they competed for land, food, and other resources. At least since the seventeenth century, the ancestors of Morning Star's Cheyennes had gradually moved west, pushed by expanding In-dian neighbors and pulled by the hunting prospects of the north-ern plains. As early as 1690, Cheyenne ancestors, who farmed the Minnesota River valley and possessed few guns, were dislodged from their homes by better-armed Sioux from the east and by Assiniboine and Cree from the north. Thus began a long history of migration for the Tsistsistas, or the People, as they called them-selves. By the early nineteenth century they had completely aban-doned village life for nomadic life and a farming economy for a hunting economy as they migrated onto the Great Plains where buffalo and antelope thrived.[21]

When the Tsistsistas moved west, they were joined by the Suhtaois —a band whose dialect the Tsistsistas understood, but who maintained a separate identity well into the nineteenth cen-tury. Not only did the Suhtaoi intermarry with the Cheyennes, but also they brought the Sacred Buffalo Hat. The Hat's powers guaranteed a plentiful supply of bison through its ability to renew herds. In addition, they taught the Tsistsistas the Sun Dance, Sweat Lodge, and Buffalo ceremonies—religious rites that would

21. E. Adamson Hoebel, *The Cheyennes: Indians of the Great Plains*, 4–9; Powell, *Sweet Medicine*, 1:21–25.

take on increasing importance to the tribe as they moved onto the plains of the Dakotas, Wyoming, and Montana.[22]

In the course of their forced migration westward, the Black Hills of northwest South Dakota became the spiritual mecca of the wandering Cheyennes. It was here the spirits taught Sweet Medicine, the Cheyenne culture hero, their tribal, social, and ceremonial organization. Here the Cheyenne Supreme Being gave Sweet Medicine the Sacred Arrows through which He poured his life into the lives of the tribe, uniting them not only to Himself but to each other. Further, the Sacred Arrows, as the supreme symbols and sources of male power, gave Cheyenne men power over other men and animals—in warfare and in the hunt.[23]

The period between 1830 and 1860 served as something of a stabilization period for the Northern Cheyennes. Anglo-Americans had arrived on the plains, but their major challenges for land remained in the future. Still the Cheyennes found little peace. As the various bands moved into and beyond the Black Hills, they encountered other Indians who resisted Cheyenne intrusion into what they perceived to be *their* hunting domains. To the west, in the Powder River country, the Crows and the Wind River Shoshones took exception to Cheyenne penetration of that territory. Those Cheyennes who eventually drifted into what would become eastern Colorado met new enemies—Utes, Comanches, and Kiowas. Behind them the ubiquitous Sioux kept up their expansionist drive until they occupied much of present-day South Dakota, large portions of North Dakota, Nebraska, and eastern Wyoming.[24]

As these various groups muscled and shouldered their way in and out of the Great Plains, tribes forged alliances. Between 1826 and 1840, a bitter war between two alliances—the Cheyennes and Arapahoes versus the Kiowas, Comanches, and Prairie Apaches, for example—arose at least in part over horses. But by 1840 the Cheyennes made peace with the Kiowas and Comanches in order to consolidate their position against the Pawnees and to obtain

22. Powell, *Sweet Medicine*, 1:23–25. For a general discussion of Cheyenne religion, see Hoebel, *Cheyennes*, 87–91.

23. Powell, *Sweet Medicine*, 1:xxi–xxiii.

24. Hoebel, *Cheyennes*, 9–10.

more horses. Northern bands made peace with the Sioux, who offered to join the Cheyennes in their fight against the Crows, Shoshones, and Pawnees. All of these political and diplomatic maneuvers, of course, influenced Indian–Anglo-American relations and certainly had ramifications for the Northern Cheyennes in autumn 1876.[25]

The roots of the 1876 Sioux War, of course, go back several decades before Private Smith met Cheyenne men on a Wyoming battlefield, to a time when Anglo-Americans traversed the Great Plains to reach Oregon's rich river valleys and California's gold. By 1851 the United States government had concluded it was essential to assure safe passage for these transcontinental travelers passing through Indian lands. The Treaty of Fort Laramie, 1851, attempted to assign at least vaguely outlined boundaries to particular tribes occupying the plains and to obtain their promise to permit travel along several overland trails. The Cheyennes and Arapahoes were assigned an area between the North Platte and Arkansas rivers, beginning at the Red Buttes on the east and going west to the "main range of the Rocky Mountains," and from the Arkansas River crossing of the Santa Fe Trail northwest to the forks of the Platte.[26] Southern bands of Cheyenne had moved down to the Arkansas River earlier in the century, while the Northern bands usually hunted and camped above the Platte. Gradually the Southern and Northern bands had developed into two distinctive groups who shared language, traditions, and family ties but had increasingly different experiences and, consequently, identities.

All went fairly well as long as Anglo-Americans in Indian country kept moving. But when they turned acquisitive eyes on the mineral resources of Colorado and Montana, matters changed considerably. The Pike's Peak Gold Rush of 1858 spelled trouble for the Southern Cheyennes in Colorado, for example. In the years that followed, tensions escalated into war between the

25. Richard White, "The Winning of the West: The Expansion of the Western Sioux in the Eighteenth and Nineteenth Centuries," *Journal of American History* 65 (Sept. 1978): 320; Elliott West, *The Contested Plains*; Hoebel, *Cheyennes*, 10; Grinnell, *Fighting Cheyennes*, 37.

26. Hoebel, *Cheyennes*, 10–11; Donald Berthrong, *The Southern Cheyennes*, 121.

Cheyennes and Arapahoes, on the one hand, and American settlers on the other. The conflict reached its bloodiest moment when Colorado Volunteers attacked a Southern Cheyenne village on Sand Creek in 1864, slaughtering women, children, and old men as well as warriors. Some Southern Cheyennes fled to their Northern friends and families with tales of the atrocities. In the meantime, a series of treaties and wars led to the eventual removal of the Southern Cheyennes and Arapahoes to a reservation in Indian Territory, later the state of Oklahoma.[27]

Like their Southern brethren, the Northern Cheyennes were not spared the confounding presence of American gold seekers. In 1863 a Georgian named John Bozeman began leading parties of miners and emigrants up a trail fashioned "the Bozeman Trail" to the gold mines of Montana. This trail crossed the Powder River country. Sioux, Cheyenne, and Northern Arapahoe resistance to further traffic on the Bozeman Trail became immediately apparent, but the United States responded by establishing a string of army posts along the road to provide protection for its users. "Red Cloud's War" was on.[28]

The details of that protracted conflict have been chronicled many times before. Suffice it to say that by 1868 the government withdrew from the Powder River country and appealed to Sioux and Cheyenne leaders to negotiate a peace. On May 10, 1868, Little Wolf, who was Sweet Medicine Chief of the Northern Cheyennes, and Morning Star (Dull Knife), along with other Cheyennes, met with peace commissioners at Fort Laramie. The Indians demanded the forts be closed. They also asked that Fort Phil Kearny (one of the posts) become an agency for the Northern Cheyennes where they could receive trade goods. And, of course, they expressed their determination to remain in the Powder River country.[29]

When Little Wolf and the others signed the treaty, then, it was with the belief the agreement conceded these demands. The actual treaty, however, made no mention of the boundaries that the Northern Cheyennes understood as part of the agreement. In-

27. Berthrong, *Southern Cheyennes*, 195–244.

28. Sherry L. Smith, "The Bozeman: Trail to Death and Glory," *Annals of Wyoming* 55 (Spring 1983): 36–42.

29. Peter J. Powell, *People* 2:766.

stead, the treaty maintained that the Northern Cheyennes and Northern Arapahoes accepted for their home a part of the Southern Cheyenne and Southern Arapahoe reservation in Indian Territory; or they could accept some portion of the country designated as the permanent home for the Brulé Sioux and other Lakota in Dakota Territory, as agreed by them in the treaty signed on April 29, 1868. Further, the actual treaty made no mention of a separate trading post for the Northern Cheyennes at the site of Fort Phil Kearny.[30]

Unaware of the contrast between their view of the agreement and the actual treaty, Little Wolf and the others returned to the main Cheyenne village. Upon reporting the treaty news, however, these men found other chiefs angry with them for signing an agreement without the consent of the entire Council of Forty-Four who governed them. In addition, any treaty would have to be blessed and ratified by the offering of the Sacred Arrow ceremonies, and the Arrows were far to the south. Unlike the proceedings of 1851, where both of these critically important conditions had been met, both were absent in 1868. Consequently, according to historian Peter Powell, a good number of Northern Cheyenne chiefs rejected the treaty and did not consider it binding upon them.[31]

They were not immediately forced to relocate, however, and in subsequent years the Northern Cheyennes continued to press their claims to the north country and their desire for traders near their home. During an 1870 meeting with emissaries from Washington, D.C., Morning Star indicated the Northern Cheyennes did not want to be completely united with the Lakotas nor have the same trading post, since the two tribes did not always agree. When the United States established Red Cloud Agency for the Sioux, Cheyenne leaders continued to resist the idea of sharing an agency.[32] Federal officials, however, were increasingly concerned not with Cheyenne wishes, but with extinguishing Cheyenne and other Indian titles to the Northern Plains, once and for all.

By 1871 the commissioner of Indian affairs had set forth a new proposition wherein Sioux, Northern Cheyennes and Northern

30. Ibid., 766.
31. Ibid., 766.
32. Ibid., 791–92.

Arapahoes would altogether give up their lands in Nebraska, Montana, and Wyoming. To this purpose government officials summoned some Northern Cheyenne leaders, including Little Wolf, Morning Star, and Spotted Wolf to Washington, D.C. in autumn 1873. There President Ulysses Grant informed them they were bound by the Treaty of 1868 to join their kinsmen in Indian Territory. The Northern Cheyennes replied that had not been their understanding of the treaty, repeated their desire to remain in the north, and left with promises to discuss these matters with their tribe when they returned home. The Council of Forty-four Chiefs, of course, rejected the idea of moving south.[33]

At that point the agent at Red Cloud received word from Washington that no more Northern Cheyennes, who had been coming into the agency for rations over the previous years, were to receive rations until their leaders agreed to move south. They would be starved into submission. In response, the bands scattered, many going to the Black Hills, others heading for Yellowstone River country, in an attempt to find sufficient food. As tensions mounted, Agent J. J. Saville requested a military post near Red Cloud, and the army established Camp, later Fort, Robinson in March 1874.

While the government marshalled its military forces, the Cheyennes looked to their sustenance as well as to their spiritual and political needs. During the summer of 1874 all the Northern Cheyennes gathered for the Sun Dance and for a renewal of the Council Chiefs. Now that the Southern People had been forced to accept a reservation far away, the Northern Chiefs knew the old Council of Forty-four, representing one united tribe, could no longer exist. So they proceeded to elect their own Council of Forty-four, which would function independently of the Council Chiefs chosen by the Southern Cheyennes. Little Wolf remained Sweet Medicine Chief. He was also named one of the four Old Man Chiefs along with Morning Star, Old Bear, and Black Moccasin, or Limber Lance, as he was also known. All maintained their commitment to remain in the Powder River country and carry on their lives as plainsmen and hunters.[34]

33. Ibid., 828–29.
34. Ibid., 924.

In the meantime, one other event of that summer affected the fate of these people. A column under the command of Lieutenant Colonel George Armstrong Custer snaked its way through the Black Hills, which was indisputably part of the Great Sioux Reservation that had been delineated by the 1868 Fort Laramie Treaty. Public sentiment favored opening up the Black Hills to non-Indians to explore rumors of its great mineral wealth. General Philip Sheridan, President Grant, and the secretaries of War and the Interior planned the 1874 Black Hills Expedition. Its purpose was to locate a site for a military post. But two "practical miners" accompanied Custer's expedition as well. They found evidence of gold and by the next spring miners flowed into the hills. While army troops attempted to expel these trespassers, the government's ultimate intentions became apparent when commissioners approached the Sioux and Northern Cheyennes about selling the Black Hills and the Powder River country, which was defined in 1868 as "unceded Indian territory" where white trespass would not be allowed without Indian consent. Some representatives from both tribes were willing to sell; others were adamantly opposed and ready to fight, if necessary, to keep that country.

On November 3, 1875, Generals Sheridan and George Crook, President Grant, and others met at the White House. They decided to stop expelling white miners from the Black Hills and to reduce the Indians' abilities to obstruct Black Hills settlements by forcing them out of the unceded hunting territories and onto areas of the Great Sioux Reservation where their raiding could be better controlled. As negotiations for the sales broke down, the commissioner of Indian affairs issued an order to the new agent at Red Cloud on December 6, 1875. He was to inform the Sioux and others still away from the government agencies they must move into their agencies by January 31, 1876, or be considered "hostile" and thus subject to military action. Most of the Northern Cheyennes had spent the winter on the lower Powder River near the Yellowstone and probably never received word of the ultimatum. Severe blizzards would have made compliance virtually impossible. Most of all, a good number of them would have seen no reason to leave their homes, for they had not broken any treaties, or any peace. From the date in the ultimatum, however, the

United States Army would treat the Northern Cheyennes living away from the agencies as "hostiles." [35]

The year 1876 was not a particularly good one for the army in Indian country. A spring campaign under the command of General George Crook included an attack on a Cheyenne camp along the Powder River. The village was burned, but the battle was something of a stalemate and the night following the fight, Cheyenne "wolves," as they called their own scouts, recaptured most of the horses lost to the troops earlier in the day. [36]

In June the army tried again. Three giant columns of troops converged upon the non-agency Sioux, Northern Cheyennes, and remnants of other tribes, who had gathered in southeastern Montana. Crook approached from the south, via the Bozeman Trail. Some of his men encountered the enemy on June 17, 1876, on the Rosebud, but failed to achieve a convincing victory. Crook moved to the vicinity of present-day Sheridan, Wyoming, to lick his wounds. Meanwhile, Colonel John Gibbon's column traveled through Montana in an easterly direction, and General Alfred Terry's men, including the flamboyant Lieutenant Colonel George A. Custer and his Seventh Cavalry, approached from the east. [37]

Without doubt, no single battle of the Indian Wars has achieved as much attention as that of June 25, 1876, on the Little Bighorn River. Most of the Northern Cheyenne Council Chiefs were in the gigantic village along that stream when Custer's soldiers attacked, although Little Wolf and Morning Star were absent. It was here, in the North Country, that the Cheyennes had decided to make *their* last stand. According to one historian of the Northern Cheyennes, "The anger that the Northern People felt against these soldiers was a terrible one—a righteous anger against these whites who had come to attack them while they were keeping peace. . . . Now all that anger that had accumulated throughout these past winters of soldier killings was turned against these troopers. They had come to kill the [Cheyennes] and their Lakota allies, but they had, instead, been killed by them." [38]

35. Ibid., 935–945; Utley, *Frontier Regulars*, 134–35, 243–244; and Hutton, *Phil Sheridan*, 166–69, 298–300.

36. John S. Gray, *Centennial Campaign: The Sioux War of 1876*, 47–58.

37. Ibid., 72–150.

38. Powell, *People* 2:1029.

It was a disastrous defeat for the soldiers in blue and the United States Army wanted revenge. That would come, military strategists hoped, if troops occupied the game country of the Yellowstone valley and the Powder River Country while simultaneously controlling the Indian agencies. Army forces in the hunting grounds would continually harass the Indians and ultimately compel their surrender at the agencies. There, under military control, they would be disarmed, dismounted, and placed on restricted reservations either to learn the white man's ways or to perish— for many nineteenth century Americans believed acculturation provided Indians their only chance for survival. At the same time, their former hunting grounds would become part of the United States public domain and eventually support Anglo-American farmers and ranchers. As part of this policy, soldiers under Captain Anson Mills's command attacked a Sioux camp of about thirty-seven lodges in what became known as the Battle of Slim Buttes, on September 9, 1876. A Sioux leader named American Horse died in the fight, but for the most part, according to historian Robert Utley, the "summer campaign of 1876 came to an unheroic conclusion."[39]

As summer was drifting into fall, General Sheridan began efforts to disarm and dismount all the Sioux, including the Oglalas already at Red Cloud Agency. Part of the responsibility for this job fell to Colonel Ranald Mackenzie, who had arrived from Fort Sill on August 17.[40] In September, Crook informed Mackenzie that his first order of business was to disarm and dismount the Sioux bands under Red Cloud and Red Leaf who lived in the vicinity of Camp Robinson in order to prevent their escape to the "hostiles." On October 22 and 23 this was accomplished. But to Sheridan's disgust, General Crook did not disarm and dismount all of the other Sioux at the agency. In addition, Crook, an advocate of using Indians against Indians in this kind of warfare, enrolled about five hundred of the Sioux for the fall campaign.[41] As

39. Utley, *Frontier Regulars*, 270–71. See also Jerome A. Greene, *Slim Buttes, 1876: An Episode of the Great Sioux War*.

40. Hutton, *Phil Sheridan*, 322–23.

41. Hutton, *Phil Sheridan*, 325; Oct. 12, 1876, telegram from Crook to Lt. Gen. Philip Sheridan from Camp Robinson, informing Sheridan that Red Cloud and Red Leaf's bands were surrounded, disarmed, and their ponies taken away,

preparations for the Powder River Expedition continued, Sioux, Shoshones, Pawnees, and even some Cheyennes signed on.

The campaign was, then, a multicultural affair, far more complicated than simply Indian versus white. The total strength of the expedition consisted of about fifteen hundred white men and about four hundred Indian auxiliaries—Sioux, Arapahoes, Shoshones, Bannocks, Pawnees, and more devastating, even a few Cheyennes.[42] What motivated these Native Americans to pick up arms against other Indians and, in some cases, their own kinsmen? The answers do not come easily, although the speeches Indian scouts made in councils with General Crook offer some insight. In addition, a few participants of the expedition, and historians since, have offered some possible explanations.

Billy Garnett, a half-blood interpreter for the army in 1876 (his mother was Sioux, his father an army officer), later explained that the Sioux enlisted because, " . . . the young men, showing wisdom beyond their years . . . had resolved by wise and firm conduct to put their nation upon a better footing in the estimation of the [United States]; and what followed with Crook was in pursuance of this sage plan."[43] To scout for the army, even against other Sioux, Garnett seemed to suggest, could be construed as a pro-Sioux act. Cooperation rather than conflict might alter white perceptions of the Sioux and lead to a stronger bargaining position in future negotiations.

An historian has recently made a similar case for some of the

---

Box 17, RG 393, Division of the Missouri, Special File, Sioux War, 1876, NARS. See also George E. Hyde, *Red Cloud's Folk: A History of the Oglala Sioux Indians*, 284–85; James C. Olson, *Red Cloud and the Sioux Problem*, 232–33; and Richmond L. Clow, "General Philip Sheridan's Legacy: The Sioux Pony Campaign of 1876," *Nebraska History* 57 (Winter 1976): 461–77.

42. Capt. John G. Bourke, *Mackenzie's Last Fight with the Cheyennes: A Winter Campaign in Wyoming and Montana*, 4.

43. "Survey Notes, William Garnett," Tablet 1, 95. George Hyde suggests that Gen. Crook practically forced the agency Sioux to scout for the army during the Powder River Campaign and that the Oglalas did not respond very heartily to his appeal for their enlistment. See Hyde, *Red Cloud's Folk*, 286–87. James Olson, however, found Crook was "highly successful in recruiting" scouts at the Red Cloud and Spotted Tail agencies, although he does not offer an explanation of the scouts' motivations. See also Olson, *Red Cloud and the Sioux Problem*, 235.

Cheyenne scouts. The exact number of Cheyenne participants remains a matter of conjecture. Included among them, however, was William Rowland, who had married a Southern Cheyenne woman in Colorado, and three of his brothers-in-law—Hard Robe, Roan Bear, and Little Fish (or Fisher). Between four and seven Northern Cheyennes also accompanied the troops to Morning Star's village, including Old Crow, Thundercloud, Blown Away, and Bird.[44] Of these, Old Crow was the most prominent, for he served in the Council of Forty-four and had traveled to Washington, D.C., in 1873 with other delegates from the tribe. While the Southern Cheyennes may not have felt ties of loyalty to the Northern People, Old Crow certainly must have. It is possible he was forced to accompany the soldiers, who understood that his presence at the battlefield could prove demoralizing for the Northern Cheyennes. It is also possible that Crook convinced Old Crow that his presence might save lives on both sides if he encouraged friends and family to surrender rather than fight. Finally, Old Crow may have seen his willingness to cooperate on this expedition as a future bargaining chip with policy makers when the time came to assign the Northern Cheyennes an agency and a reservation of their own. What could give the appearance of treachery and betrayal, in other words, might have been an attempt to salvage tribal goals under extremely adverse circumstances.[45]

Pawnee and Shoshone men, on the other hand, did not have to grapple with concerns of treachery or betrayal, for they had long viewed the Sioux and Cheyennes as their enemies. Tribal identities superseded any sense of racial solidarity, and the rapid, aggressive expansion of the latter tribes onto the plains in the late eighteenth and the early nineteenth century had deepened the differences. Intertribal warfare—fought largely for social and economic benefits, including better hunting grounds and horses—characterized Indian-Indian relations long before Anglo-

44. Powell, *Sweet Medicine* 1:144; Powell, *People* 2:1060; Karen Easton, "Getting Into Uniform: Northern Cheyenne Scouts in the United States Army, 1876–81," (master's thesis, University of Wyoming, 1985), 34–35. See also Stands in Timber, *Cheyenne Memories*, 214.

45. Easton, "Getting Into Uniform," 36–46, 129.

Americans entered the competition for the northern plains. So, when white scout Frank North received an order from General Philip Sheridan to enlist one hundred Pawnee scouts for an autumn campaign against the Sioux, he had no trouble finding volunteers. Not only were they willing to fight their old foe, the Sioux, but they were also anxious to flee their own reservation in Indian Territory, where many suffered from ague. In addition, the Pawnees longed to return to their homeland, and enlisting in the army provided one of the few escapes from the misery of their lives at the agency.[46]

Official plans for the Sioux and the Northern Cheyennes, meanwhile, were clearly laid out in a telegram Sheridan sent General William T. Sherman on the eve of this campaign. Once the Indians were "Disarmed and dismounted," he wrote, "[the problem] would reduce itself to a simple question of feeding them till they learn to raise some food for themselves. Meantime miners and settlers will fill up north of Laramie & about the Black Hills so that these troublesome Indians would be hemmed in and

46. North, *Man of the Plains*, 197–98. For a general discussion of Indian scouts' motivations, see Thomas W. Dunlay, *Wolves for the Blue Soldiers: Indian Scouts and Auxiliaries with the United States Army, 1860–1890*, 108–26. Richard White explains the dynamics of intertribal warfare and its connection to the Indian scouts issue this way: "From the perspective of most northern and central plains tribes the crucial invasion of the plains during this period was not necessarily that of the whites at all. These tribes had few illusions about American whites and the dangers they presented, but the Sioux remained their most feared enemy. . . . Even as they fought the Americans, the Sioux continued to expand their domination of plains hunting grounds, as they had to in order to survive. Logically enough, the tribes the Sioux threatened—the Crows, Pawnees and Arikaras especially—sided with the Americans, providing them with soldiers and scouts. For white historians to cast these people as mere dupes or traitors is too simplistic. They fought for their tribal interests and loyalties as did the Sioux." See White, "The Winning of the West," 320–21, 342. For more information on the Pawnee scouts, see "Pawnee Trails and Trailers: An Important Chapter in the Geography and History of the Old West," *Motor Travel Magazine* (March 1929): 10–13; (April 1929): 11–14; (May 1929): 11–14; (June 1929): 8–11; (July 1929): 5–7; (Aug. 1929): 17–20; (Sept. 1929): 9–13; (Oct. 1929): 16–19; (Dec. 1929): 16–18; (Jan. 1930): 20–21; (Feb. 1930): 17–20; and (March 1930): 17–20; and Thomas R. Buecker and R. Eli Paul, "The Pawnee Scouts Mounted Auxiliaries, 1864–1877," *Military Images* 7 (July–Aug. 1985), 16–19.

would gradually become like those in Minnesota."[47] Of generals'
plans and policies, the Northern Cheyennes who hunted through
the summer days of 1876 knew precious little. The same could be
said for Private William Earl Smith. Yet before year's end, the
decisions of distant people brought these Cheyennes, Smith, and
his fellow soldiers to battle. For Earl the experience began at
Camp Robinson, Nebraska.

47. Sheridan to Sherman, Nov. 10, 1876, Box 17, RG 393, Division of the
Missouri, Special File, Sioux War, 1876, NARS.

CHAPTER 2

Preparations for War

Earl's account of the Powder River Expedition begins on an undated fragment of paper, at mid-sentence. It is possible the lost
pages include an account of disarming the Sioux bands near Camp
Robinson and that these are the "prisners" to which he refers. At
any rate, the diary commences with Smith returning to camp on
horseback. He evidently nodded off and dreamed of home:

October 1876

. . . dreams I ever had. I would think some times I was at home
and was jest a going to set down to a good meal and then the horse
would stumble and then I would wake up with a curse to find it
was all a lie and then I would try to keep a wake and watch the
rest [of the men]. Some would fall asleep and their horses would
wonder out of colom and then you could hear the offisers cusing
them. Well we come to Camp Robinson about two Oclock in the
nite and turned our Prisners over at the Post and then went down
to our quarters and the men that were left back had a kind of a
supper reddy for us and some eate and some went to bed. As for
myself I eate till I made my self sick. And it was near day brake
when I fell asleep sitting by the stove.

I will not state what happened between this date and the 31st
Oct. I was ordered to reporte to him [Colonel Ranald Mackenzie]
for Ordlay for the Scoute. We had muster on that day and so after
it I took my bundel of bedding and my horse and went up to the

Post and reported to Gen. McKinsey.[1] He asked me my name and some few more questions and told me to report to Sargent Magor Welch [Walsh] as one of the ordleys witch I did. I will now say this Sargent Mager was an grate big overgrown Irshman and I did not like the new thing much but I was kind of green a round hed quarters and did not have any thing to say. I waited out Side for a little while and the first saloot I goot [got] from the Sargint mager was God dam you Soul bee a little lively a round hear. I node I was pooty [pretty] lively on foot So I took it all in and sed nothing. I will not Say any more hear but we drawd raishons for ten days. And then went back to the quarters and Slept all nite

The first day of the winter campaign, or "scout" as Smith called it, was notable for the disorder that accompanied it. While the men were en route to Fort Laramie they apparently felt no concern about Indian attack, making the chaos safe and consequently tolerable, if not desirable.

Winter Scout for Nov. 1st, 1876

I saddoled up in the morning and went up to hed quarters a[nd] started to pack up the Genrals things in a Wagon. When his things were all in our things had to go in the same wagon. Well we had an eight mule wagon and the Genral say Pack it fool [full]. And after we goot every thing in we had no room for our tents and we had to strap them on the out side and it made a pooty [pretty] big lode. Well by this time the company had come out and the Genral gave them orders to start out on our roade. Well we did not start till after all the rest had gone and then the Genral and all us ordeleys started. Eleven all told [were] on the Staff.

By this time it had goot to bee near 12 Oclock. Well of course we had not had our dinner. Well we marched down threw the White Eerth Cannon [White River] passing the wagons and then past all the command. Well we come to the end at last, 18 mils out. There is a fine Stream in this Cannon and we had to cross it 24 times and that made it slow travling for the wagons. Well it was Sun down when we goot to comt [camp] and it was after dark when all the command goot in. You see our command cossisted of

1. Throughout his diary, Smith refers to Mackenzie by his brevet or honorary rank of general. For officers and others to use the honorary title was common practice in the nineteenth century.

9 companys of cavalry 5 of Infantry and 4 of Artillery.[2] Well then the word went a round, where is the wagons? No wagons no supper. And so it went on till 10 Oclock and the first wagon come in. But it was not ours and the Genral began to walk a round for our Wagon had out [ought] to bee a hed [of the one that had already arrived].

We had a fire for it was pooty cold. I was gitting all the comfort I could out of the fire when I hird the Genral call out Smith. My name had goot to bee pooty common all reddy. Well I goot up and went to him nearly starved. He says jump on your horse and go back and do not stop till you find Leut. Latton [Henry Lawton][3]

2. According to Lt. Bourke, the "expedition was composed of eleven companies of cavalry, from the 2d, 3d, 4th and 5th regiments, under command of General Ranald S. Mackenzie; four companies of the 4th Artillery, dismounted, and eleven companies of infantry, from the 4th, 9th, 14th and 23rd regiments, under Colonel R. I. Dodge." See Bourke, *Mackenzie's Last*, 3. Col. Richard I. Dodge enumerated the force somewhat differently in his diary: "McKenzie [*sic*] has 13 companies of Cavalry—divided into three battalions—I have 4 Companies of Artillery and 11 Companies of Infantry—divided into two battalions." See Richard I. Dodge diary, Nov. 14, 1876, Richard Irving Dodge Papers, Newberry Library.

3. Lt. Henry Lawton was born in Manhattan, Ohio, in 1843, making him 36 years old during the Powder River Campaign. Like so many other men in the post–Civil War army, his military career began with that conflict. When the war began, Lawton lived in Fort Wayne, Ind., where he was working in a law office. On April 16, 1861, Lawton enlisted in the 9th Indiana Volunteers. After serving 3 months, he was mustered out and immediately organized the 30th Indiana Volunteers, becoming first lieutenant of Company A. By the end of the war he had reached the rank of lieutenant colonel (Volunteers) and was offered a commission as second lieutenant in the regular army. Lawton chose to attend Harvard Law School instead, yet in April 1867 he asked that the commission be tendered again, and this time he accepted it. By July, Lawton was promoted to first lieutenant and in Jan. 1871 he was transferred to the Fourth Cavalry. It was not until 3 years after the Powder River Campaign that he gained a captaincy, and it was an additional 10 years before he became major and inspector general. Lawton's last regular army appointment came in July 1898, when he was promoted to colonel and inspector general. In the meantime, however, he volunteered to fight in the Spanish-American War, receiving appointment first as brigadier general of the Volunteers in May 1898, and then major general in July 1898. Lawton was killed in action at San Mateo, Philippine Islands, on Dec. 19, 1899.

In a brief autobiographical statement about his military career Lawton had the following to say about the Powder River Campaign and his part in it: "After

for he had charge of the wagon train and tell him to git our wagon in as soon as posibale [and] to let it pass the rest of the wagons if it was behind. I mounted up with out a saddle and started out on the jump. I did not come on to any wagon for a bout 3 mils and I had as good a horse as there was in the command and I had not broke the lope yet. And I did not stop hear went on a bout 1 mile and hear found one wagon unloded for the muls [mules] could not pool [pull it] up the hill. I was pooty worm by this time and the horse to so I stoped and hird [heard] the teamster curse a while.

I went on a little father and hear found a wagon broke down   there was some doe boys [infantry] around this wagon. I did not think it was safe to stay a round this croud for they were like mad men and so I went on and found wagons in the same fix for a bout 2 mils. I then come to the Leut. and told him what the Genroll sed. He told me to go back and tell the Genrol he did not now [know] what time he could git to camp and to tell him just how things were a long the road. He asked me how far it was to camp and I told him I thought it was a bout 6 mils. He then aferd me a drink out of a bottle but I told him I never drank. I started back on the jump and never pooled up till I come to camp for it was moon light and could se well. I told the Genral all I had found out and went down where the boys were and they had borrowd some flour and bacon and coffe from one of the wagons that had come in so they had made flap jacks. So I took the pan for they were all done eating and it was fun to see me eate for I had not had a bite since earley in the morning. The Sargent Mager had to poot in and says you eate like a dam hog but I sed nothing. Well I goot done and made down my bed that is I roled up in my Saddle blanket and took my saddle for a pillow and never woke up till the bugle sounded revilee.

---

the disaster to General Custer and his command on the Little Big Horn in the summer of 1876, I applied to be relieved from recruiting duty, and to be allowed to join the troops ordered to that Department, which was granted, and I took part in the campaigns and marches of that command, including the severe winter campaign in Wyoming, and in the battle with the Cheyennes, Nov. 25, 1876, resulting in their defeat, the entire destruction of their camp, and their final surrender." See "Military History of the Late General Henry W. Lawton," Jan. 15, 1892, Henry W. Lawton, Military Service Record, File #812 ACP 1881, Box 708, RG 94, Records of the Adjutant General's Office, NARS. See also Francis B. Heitman, *Historical Register and Dictionary of the United States Army*, 620.

Thursday Nov 2st, 1876

Our wagon had come in by this time and we unlodad and goot our breakfast and packed up a gane [again] and left this camp. We were all to geather now a gane and we were at the hed. We marched 12 mils and went into camp on Running Wotter after the horses were all turned out to hird and our tents up the Genrall says Smith go over to Mager Mack [Captain Clarence Mauck][4] and tell him to poot his hird over there pointing with his finger. I went to the Magor and says the Genrall say poot your hird over there jest as the General had done. He says dose he mean over the crick I says I don't [k]now Sir. Then he say, God dam your Soul if you ever come to me that way a gane I will make you walk all the trip. My hair stood up strate I [k]now but I dare not say a word. and walked a way like a whiped school boy. I [k]now at the time I would [have] gave five years of my life to [have] walked up to him and smaked him in the nose. There was no wood at this camp and the boys began to tare down an old stable that is at an ranch hear. It was here at this camp that the two companies of Indians first camped with us.[5]

Friday Nov. 3d, 1876

Left camp at nine Oclock and marched 25 miles to Rawhide creek and camped. It was at the crossing of this creek that only three months before the Indians burnt the ranche, killed one man and two escaped. Not being much wood here I had to carry a log as heavy as myself for a bout one mile. The men had to come to hed

4. Clarence Mauck first joined the U.S. Army in March 1861, when he received a commission as 2nd lt. in the 1st Cavalry. Several months later he became 1st lt. and in Aug. 1861 transferred to the Fourth Cavalry. This Indiana-born officer attained the rank of captain in 1863 and remained at that level until 1879, when he became a major in the 9th Cavalry. He died 2 years later of consumption, at age 40. Mauck was 35 during the Powder River Campaign of 1876. See Clarence Mauck, Military Service Record, File #436 ACP 1877, RG 94, Records of the Adjutant General's Office, NARS; Heitman, *Historical Register*, 697.

5. These were probably the Sioux scouts. It is interesting to note that throughout his account Smith uses the same word, "Indians," to identify both those people who cooperated with the army on this expedition and those who were the enemy. Considerable interest in the Indian scouts among the general public is evident in the frequent newspaper articles about them in the *Cheyenne Daily Leader*. See issues dated Aug. 8, 11; Oct. 25, 31; Nov. 11, 18, 21, and 24; and Dec. 20, 1876.

quarters and git their forrige and you could hear grate growling for they had to correy it a long ways to there companys.

Saturday, Nov. 4th, 1876

We broke camp earley and made 28 mils and camped on North Plat[te] River a bout 1 mile above Fort Learmie [Laramie].[6] We got in to camp pooty late and goot our tents up and all fixed. I went to bed earley and went to sleep for the nite as I supposed but that was not to bee. About 10 Oclick I hird that handy name Smith. I jumped up and drested and went out only to meet that noted Sergent Mager with God dam your lasy Sole! It takes you longer to dress than it would a holl company. Now says he go and saddle up your hors and the Generals to and report to him. Of corse I felt good after beeing so kindly talk[ed] to and goot the horses and went to the tent. Then the Genrall come out and we mounted up and started to the fort. It was about 11 Oclock now and the Genral jumped off and says Look out for the horses. Well there I stood I gess about two ours [hours]. Then I saw some one come out the dore and come up to my [me]. I now thought I would bee back Soon in my tent under my blankets.[7] But at lass [alas] it was not to bee so for in stid [instead] of beeing the genral it was one of General Crooks ordleys with a drink of whiskey for me but I told him no I did not wont it all thoe [although] it went a gane [against] the grane.

I was nearley frose by this time and I asked him how long he thought it would bee before he would come out. God only [k]nows says he they air [are] all pooty fool [full]. We talk a while and then he went in and left me to think of the post. I had often hird of

6. Fort Laramie was originally erected in 1834 as a trading post. The U.S. Army purchased it in 1849. The post's name derived from the Laramie River, which, in turn, was named for a French trapper, Jacques Laramie. Fort Laramie provided some protection for emigrants on the Oregon Trail during the 1850s and 1860s. See Robert W. Frazer, *Forts of the West: Military Forts and Presidios and Posts Commonly Called Forts of the Mississippi River to 1898*, 182. See also Robert A. Murray, *Military Posts of Wyoming*, 12–23.

7. According to Homer Wheeler, second lieutenant with the 5th Cavalry, each soldier was allowed 2 blankets while the expedition rested at Fort Laramie. They also received "A" tents, which 4 men shared. Tents were pitched face to face, allowing sufficient room between to place a Sibley stove. The men took turns keeping up the fires. Wood was so scarce that troopers had to gather buffalo chips and sagebrush for fuel. As for beds, they spread their blankets over mattresses made of grass and sagebrush. See Homer W. Wheeler, *The Frontier Trail, or from Cowboy to Colonel*, 170–71.

nigers standing out side and holding the horses but I never node [knowed] how it went before. Time went by and finley yes after a while I saw what was a grate Genral but a few ours [hours] befor. But now alass. Yes, alass. Well we finley goot started and I was so stiff with the cold I could hardly ride. But the way we went over that hill I soon goot warm. We were about two mints [minutes] gitting to camp.

Sunday, Nov. 5th, 1876

I had to jump up with the bugle and take care of my horse and git my brekfast. And then I heard that name Smith from the Genrall. I begon to think now that I was the only Ordley that he had all thoe [although] there was 4 more beside me. Well I went to the tent and he says git your horse and go up to the Post and give this dispatch to Gen. Crook jest as soon as you can. Well a way I went and dellivered it and started back. When I goot near back I met the Gen. all a lone. He says come with me Smith. So I followed him a round for a while and he sent me to comt [camp] with the order to pack up. Well we goot packed up and started on our march. It was hear that Gen. Crook first joined us with a nother Company of Cavelery[8] and it was on this day we felt the first of Winter [It had] Snode [snowed] some in the afternoon. We

---

8. Gen. George Crook remains one of the better-known officers of the Indian Wars. For more information see Martin F. Schmitt, ed., *General George Crook: His Autobiography*, and Jerome Greene, "George Crook," in Hutton, *Soldiers West*, 118–36. The men who fought with Crook in the West did not all agree on his skill in military matters. Col. Richard I. Dodge, as detailed below, was quite critical of Crook's organizational skills during the Powder River Campaign. On the other hand, Lt. Bourke highly respected his commander. In his published account of this expedition, Bourke compared the temperaments of Ranald Mackenzie and George Crook, noting that the former "was looked upon by the whole army as the embodiment of courage, skill and dash in an eminent degree. Impetuous, headstrong, perhaps a trifle rash, he formed a curious contrast to his self-poised, cool silent commander whom the Indians of the plains and mountains from the British line to Mexico had learned to know and respect as the 'Gray Fox.'" See John G. Bourke, *Mackenzie's Last*, 3. Pvt. James B. Frew, who participated in the Battle of Slim Buttes and the famous "Starvation March" following that fight, wrote his parents in Oct. 1876 that most of the men did not revere Crook: "I have never heard Crook's name mentioned but with a curse   the men fired into his tent   tried to kill him   he thought it was indians." See Paul L. Hedren, ed., "Campaigning with the 5th Cavalry: Private James B. Frew's Diary and Letters from the Great Sioux War of 1876," *Nebraska History* 65 (Winter 1984): 459. See also Heitman, *Historical Register*, 340.

Sharp Nose, an Arapaho scout working with the U.S. Army during the Powder River Expedition, was one of the few Indian allies Smith mentions by name. Credit: Wyoming State, Archives, Museums and Historical Department

marched 18 mils and went in to camp on the North Plot [Platte] river.

Monday Nov. 6th 1876

This day we made 18 mils all so [also] and went in to camp near North Plat on some mud hols. Hear some of the indins had found some muls and the Genral sent me over to see if they were Government muls or not. There was an Indin with me by the name of Sharp nose[9] and he started and poor me behind him. We jest flew

9. Sharp Nose was spokesman for the Arapahoe scouts who accompanied the Powder River Campaign. Billy Garnett, half-blood interpreter for the Sioux, claimed Sharp Nose was the best scout he ever knew. See "Survey Notes, Wil-

over ditches and hols. I thought he was jest trying me to see how a soldier could ride. Well now I was not to bee bluffed of by an Indine and I kept wright on to him. He kept looking back and when we goot there he says heep ride. I then made signs that they were not Guverment muls and went back. I had not been in my tent long when I hird that Sargent Mager calling Smith, Smith. I says What the hell do you want? He flew at the tent and says what do you mean by talking that way to me? He says if you ever talk to me that way a gane I will tie you up by the thumbs. [10]

Tuosday Nov. 7th 1876

We left camp at sun rise and it was offle [awful] dusty a way behind in the collom all day—marched 15 mils and went in to camp on Elk horn crick   plenty of wood hear pooty good wotter.

Wensday Nov. 8th 1876

Broke camp at 9 Oclock and march 15 mils and went in to camp on Wagon hound crick. We past eight or nine graves on the road   [People] suposed to of been kild by Indins. It was hear that the big Suply trane come in site of us and they camped about 3 mils from us and the Pawne Indins cot [caught] up hear to for the first time.

Although Private Smith failed to note it, on November 8 some of the Indian scouts met with General Crook. The best contem-

---

liam Garnett at Cane Creek, S.D., 1907," Tablet No. 1, Box 4, Eli Seavey Ricker Collection, Nebraska State Historical Society, 97. Bourke found Sharp Nose's skills as a sign-talker equally impressive: "The palm of eminence, oratorically and eloutionally, belongs to Sharp Nose; standing erect in the middle of the floor, with his red blanket draped gracefully about his loins and falling to his feet in broad folds, he impressed his listeners much more than did Three Bears and Fast Thunder who delivered themselves of their speeches, while sitting down." John G. Bourke diary, Nov. 8, 1876, 14:1371–72, microfilm copy, Denver Public Library. The original Bourke diaries are available at the United States Military Academy Library, West Point (hereafter USMA). In his published book, Bourke described Sharp Nose as tall, straight, with a large frame, piercing eyes, Roman nose, firm jaw and chin—"a face inspiring confidence in his ability and determination. His manners were dignified and commanding, coming nearer to the Fenimore Cooper style of Indian than any I had seen since my visit to 'Cocheis,' the renowned chief of the Chiricahaua Apaches, in the Dragoon Mountains, Arizona, in February, 1873." Bourke, *Mackenzie's Last*, 14.

10. For a description of this form of military punishment, see Marian Russell, *Land of Enchantment: Memoirs of Marian Russell Along the Santa Fe Trail*, 108.

porary account of the scouts' points of view comes from the diary of Lieutenant John Gregory Bourke, Crook's aide-de-camp during the Powder River Expedition. Unusually interested in Indian material cultures and customs, Bourke claimed that his "personal inclinations led [him] to associate as much as possible with our savage scouts, whose modes of life, language and religious thought were always of an indescribable interest. Nearly all the talk I had with anybody was with them and the result was the enrichment of note-books with references to aboriginal customs in war and peace which probably could not have been obtained under circumstances of greater advantage."[11]

While clearly a nineteenth century man with his ethnocentrism intact, Bourke did attempt a verbatim record of the scouts' remarks made during the November 8, 1876, council with General Crook. To be sure, these remarks came filtered through interpreters and so were subject to error. Nevertheless, while not a perfect rendering of scout sentiments, they do provide some insight. Bourke's account of the comments of the Sioux Three Bears are indicative of the scouts' concerns:[12]

---

11. Bourke, *Mackenzie's Last*, 10. Bourke's background provides few clues concerning his particular interest in Indian cultures. His parents came to the United States from Ireland as a young married couple and settled in Philadelphia, where he was born, June 23, 1846. Early in life Bourke demonstrated a love of books and studied Greek, Latin, and Gaelic. At 16 he ran away to join the army, enlisting in the 15th Pennsylvania Cavalry, where he served as private and sergeant between 1862 and 1865. After the Civil War, he attended West Point and upon graduation in 1869 accepted a commission as second lieutenant in the 3d U.S. Cavalry. For the next 15 years he served in Arizona, Montana, the Dakotas, and Wyoming. In 1880, Bourke was assigned duty as recorder of the Poncas Commission and after that was asked to investigate the manners and customs of Pueblos, Navajos, and Apaches. He returned to his unit as captain in 1882 and died June 8, 1896, in Vermont. During his career in the army he contributed articles to scientific periodicals and wrote several books on Indian warfare and cultures. He was elected president of the American Folklore Society one year before his death. See John Peters's introduction to Bourke, *Mackenzie's Last*, iv–v; Heitman, *Historical Register*, 232; Joseph C. Porter, *Paper Medicine Man: John Gregory Bourke and His American West*; and Joseph C. Porter, "John G. Bourke," in Hutton, ed., *Soldiers West*, 137–56.

12. Bourke described Three Bears as "young in years, but mature in thought. He looked, as he was, a man whose friendship could be relied on. He made no pretensions as a speaker and cut but a poor figure in declamation, when 'Sharp Nose' was in the same council. His power as a commander depended more upon

Before leaving Red Cloud Agency, I told the agent I wanted him to give our people their regular allowance of rations while we are gone on this scout. I am talking now for all our families left back to Red Cloud Agency. I want the beeves turned out the same as they ever were.

I have three things to say and that's all. When that delegation gets back from the Indian Territory [a delegation sent to look into the Territory's suitability for a Sioux reservation] I want it to wait for me and not go to Washington until we can start together. I don't want them to start before that time. As soon as we get through with this business out here, we can work together and that's the reason I want them to wait for me. Sometimes, I may want to ask for something and whenever I do, I want the General (Crook) to agree to it. When we travel together, we ought to work together as one.

A great many of our men back at the Agency have guns but no ammunition. I want to have a note sent to both those stores at the Agency to have them sell ammunition for a couple of days, because the hostile Indians will come down there and raise trouble with our people while we are away. I want you to write right away [about these demands], because if my young people don't cry for grub while I am away, I'll like you all the better when I come back.

Those things I can't get I want you to tell me now. The Pawnees have a great herd of horses here; we want half to drive along.

General Crook: All right. There'll be a fair division made.

Three Bears: I want you to put in your letter we got one half of those horses back. When you send us out on a scout, we want to work our own way.

General Crook: That's it exactly.

Three Bears: If a man wants to live in this world, he has got to do right and keep his ears straight. Then he gets along without trouble. We are going to listen to you after this and do what you tell us. If we get any money for our country (i.e., the Black Hills), we don't want it taken away from us. I want the Great Father [President] to hear me when I call for oxen, wagons and sheep and when they are given to me, I don't want the agent to keep them for me; I can keep them myself.[13]

---

the success to be won from stealthy movements and crafty combinations than from any lion-like attack such as 'Sharp Nose's' face suggested he might make." See Bourke, *Mackenzie's Last*, 14.

13. Quoted in Bourke diary, Nov. 8, 1876, 14:1367–69, USMA.

Savvy rather than "savagery" characterized the scout's remarks. The welfare of their own people uppermost in their minds, Three Bears and others clearly intended to play their enlistment for political and economic ends. Furthermore, these comments demonstrate that intertribal rivalries (in this case Sioux and Pawnee) were important in the relationships between those Indians who participated in this campaign. For the duration of the expedition, however, peaceful wariness and eventual friendliness characterized interactions among the various scouts.

In the meantime, Private Smith continued to make his way toward Fort Fetterman, the place where the entire command would organize before beginning its march up the Bozeman Trail. Fort Fetterman had gained a reputation as a hardship post in the frontier army—partly due to the severe Wyoming winters. But Lieutenant Bourke found the fort this November to be rather attractive. While its buildings offered no architectural elegance, they were in good repair, clean, and freshly painted. The walls of barracks and officers' quarters alike had been washed with a solution of lime and colored with indigo, leaving a violet or purple hue.[14] Private Smith, nevertheless, took up quarters in a tent about one mile from the fort.

Thursday Nov. 9th 1877 [1876]

Broke camp at sun rise   made 18 mils and went in to camp on [the North] Plot [Platte] River 1 mile from Fort Fetterman. Goot to camp earley and it was a nice day so I washed my close [clothes] and it turned off cold   about nite the prayery [prairie] cout [caught] fire and come near driving us out of camp. It was at this camp that the old gard had to report to poot up hed quarters tents and git wood. This took a great deal off of us ordleys. It was hear that two men of the old gard come up and reported to the Genral in this manner. Hello. What do you want us to do hear? The Gen. says look hear my man who air [are] you? They told him and then

---

14. Ibid., Nov. 11, 1876, 14:1383. Fort Fetterman was established in July 1867 on a sagebrush plateau along the south side of the North Platte River to protect various emigrant routes, including the Bozeman Trail, which left the river and swung northward at this point. The post was named for Capt. William Fetterman, killed at Fort Phil Kearny the previous December. Frazer, *Forts*, 181; see also Murray, *Military Posts*, 72–75.

This sketch of *General Crook's Headquarters, Fort Fetterman*, is one of several drawn by a *Harper's Weekly* artist who accompanied the troops. They were published in a December 1876 issue. Credit: Wyoming State Archives, Museums and Historical Department

he cold [called] a Sargent and told him to take them out and make them sulite [salute] a stump for 1 hour and a half. Then some of the gard was late and he made them correy [carry] forrige about a mile for punishment.[15]

Friday Nov. 10th 1876

We lay over all day and they had all the companys out drilling. I lay in my tent and watched them   twards nite I took a dispatch up to Gen Crook and saw some of the men pooty fool [drunk] and some were lade out.[16] Commenced snowing about 9 oclock.

15. For information on the system of military justice and on punishments meted out to enlisted men, see Coffman, *Old Army*, 375–81; Rickey, *Forty Miles*, 179–84, 253.

16. Alcoholism was clearly a major problem in the nineteenth-century army. In the 1880s, 41 for every 1,000 men in the army were hospitalized as alcoholics, and only the most severe cases were treated. Interestingly, there is no definite correlation between alcoholism and frontier service, for the lowest ratio of alcoholics at any single army post was at Fort Custer, Mont. Perhaps more than the location of post, general troop morale and officers' decorum (or lack of it) influenced the drinking habits of soldiers. See Rickey, *Forty Miles*, 156–63; Coffman, *Old Army*, 388.

Saturday Nov. 11 1876

Lay over all day   a nice day   we drawd our Seal Skin caps and over shoos hear to day.[17]

Sunday Nov. 12 1876

I woke with a shudder for I was cold   for the first I node [knowed] it was winter. I peeped out of my tent and there before my eyes I beheld a foot of snow but I had to croll [crawl] out and feed my hors and went to my brekfast—I mist [missed] one of the boys now and asked where is Wilson?[18] Now then, this Sargent Mager Welch had to poot in. He says Whot the hell is that your buisness [business]. If you don't tend to your one [own] buisnss I will make you. It is a good thing for this rum sucker that I never drank or I would [have] been apt to kill him one of those times. But I had to much sence to give back talk. Well I smelt a rat and walked up to his [Wilson's] tent and looked in   and there I saw my man with his nose split open and eye cut—he was all over blud and pooty drunk yet. I goot some warm wotter for it was offel [awful] cold and washed him off the best I could. And then I goot it out of him how it come. He sed he was cold [called] up in the nite to go up to the Fort [Fetterman] with Leut. Latton [Henry Lawton] and they both goot drunk and started to come back and his [Wilson's] hors ran a way with him. That started the Leut. hors and as he come up by his side the Leut. drew his pistell and struck him a cros the fase with it witch nocked [knocked] him off and sen[se]less. When he woke he found him self in the edge of the Plat River all wet and all blud but he went to camp and went to bed before day Broke. The Genral gave the Leut. quite a talking to, but that did not a mount to nothing as I will hereafter show. Of course he felt

17. According to Rickey, regular troops setting out on lengthy campaigns usually went in "heavy marching order." This meant, for the infantrymen, a haversack, half a "dog tent," rations, and up to 150 rounds of .45-caliber rifle ammunition. Cavalrymen's heavy marching order included most of the same materials plus horse accoutrements. Cavalrymen might also carry 10 to 15 pounds of grain for their horses. See Rickey, *Forty Miles*, 221–22. On the Powder River Campaign, fur caps were issued only to those companies likely to take the field against the enemy. Based on company reports that fur gauntlets were a worthless fraud, frequently splitting in the back due to a defect in the tanning or dyeing, Crook chose not to use them on this expedition. See General Crook to General Williams, Nov. 20, 1876, Powder River Expedition Order Book, John G. Bourke Papers, USMA, 37.

18. This was, possibly, Edward Wilson, Company F, 4th Cavalry.

sorrey when he goot strate and told Wilson if he wanted any thing
he would git it for him. Snode till noon to day   pooty cold.

Monday Nov. 13 1876

Still we lay over for orders to move on   very cold all day. This
morning the frost stood out on everything. The Gen. Stade up
with Gen. Crook all nite and I took his horse up to him in the
morning and we come back. We had not been back long when I
hird that affle [awful] name Smith. I did hate to leave that little
Sibley Stove for it was nice and warm in the tent. Well I went out
and this Sargent Mager says saddle up your one and the Genrals
hors   so I done so and went to the Gen. He come out and
mounted and we started. He says to me Smith how dose your little
hors run. Well I says he ollways keeps up with the rest of them.
Well he says that is a good horse and we will have a rase [race].
Well we started. We jest flew for a half of a mile. I could of past
him but I did not like to. Well we stade there about an our [hour]
and come back   the old man felt his Bitters pooty well and we
come back as fast as we went and I liked it for it was fearful cold.[19]

While Smith sought the warmth of his precious Sibley stove
and undoubtedly brooded over the treatment enlisted men received at the hands of belligerent sergeant majors and intoxicated
lieutenants, officers made preparations for the march. Clothing,
ordnance, forage, and ammunition had to be gathered and new
recruits had to be drilled. They also discussed news brought over
the telegraph line—most provocative news was the close and con-
troversial presidential election of 1876, which matched Rutherford B. Hayes against Samuel Tilden. Even at remote frontier
posts this contest generated excitement over charges of irregulari-
ties in three southern states' election procedures. Eventually, Congress settled the conflict with a compromise—the Republicans
gained the presidency while the southern Democrats gained the
end of Reconstruction—but not before there was renewed talk of
civil war. To Lieutenant John Bourke, "Such news is more grave

19. Horse racing was evidently a popular sport among frontier soldiers. According to Homer Wheeler, who participated in the Powder River Expedition,
every company of cavalry had a horse the men thought could run and they were
always willing to back their favorite with hard cash. In this way the men had
some exciting races and found some amusement. See Wheeler, *Frontier Trail*,
164.

than would be an intimation of hostilities with foreign nations; internecine wars are always the most frightful and most costly, excepting always those having an infusion of religious fanaticism. Severe as our coming experiences may be, they will be more welcome than a campaign in the Sunny lands of the South against our own misguided people." [20]

Lieutenant Colonel Richard Irving Dodge,[21] who would command the battalions of infantry and artillery on the Powder River Expedition, also noted this political event in his diary—describing it as "bad" news while prophesying, "Looks like a row." [22] Dodge had arrived at Fort Fetterman on November 10, after he received Crook's offer to command the infantry. He traveled by rail from Omaha to Medicine Bow and then marched to Fetterman—a trip notably different from Private Smith's, for it included "a most luxurious bath" while camped on Twelve Mile Spring; "a rare luxury," Dodge admitted, while "camping out." [23] Once at the post, he passed the time signing papers, getting the command properly set up, renewing old acquaintances and making new ones among the officers, playing billiards, and seeing to his own comfort while on the trail. That included acquiring a splendid tent, a trestle for his bed so that he would not have to sleep on the ground, four camp stools, two tables, and a leather-

20. Bourke diary, Nov. 11, 1876, 14:1380.

21. Richard Irving Dodge was born in Huntsville, N.C., and in 1844 received an appointment to West Point. After graduating nineteenth in his class, he was assigned to the 8th Infantry as a second lieutenant in Dec. 1848. By the time of the Civil War, Dodge had achieved a captaincy and at the conclusion of the war was a major in the 12th Infantry. His next promotion came 9 years later, when Dodge became lieutenant colonel of the 23d Infantry, the rank he held during the Powder River Campaign. He was 49 years old in the autumn of 1876 and on the verge of publishing his book *The Plains of the Great West and Their Inhabitants*. In 1882, Dodge published another book, *Our Wild Indians*. That year was also notable for him because he was promoted to colonel of the 11th Infantry. He retired in that rank May 1891 and died June 16, 1895. See the unpublished brief biography by Don Russell, Folder 3, Box 1, Richard Irving Dodge Papers, Newberry Library. See also Richard Irving Dodge Military Service Record, File #4425 ACP 1873, Box 209, RG 94, Records of the Adjutant General's Office, NARS, and Heitman, *Historical Register*, 377.

22. Dodge diary, Nov. 11, 1876, Richard Irving Dodge Papers, Newberry Library.

23. Ibid., Nov. 8, 1876.

backed chair.[24] An enlisted man settled for two blankets, the hard ground, and one tent he shared with four others.[25]

So outfitted, the gathering force that became the Powder River Expedition paused on the banks of the North Platte River. Some probably gazed toward Indian country, and perhaps the more poetic found the landscape compelling. On the day Private Smith curtly mentioned drawing his sealskin cap and overshoes, Lieutenant Bourke waxed eloquent on the countryside:

Far away to the distant horizon, the white-mantled terraces, extended on ridge upon ridge until they touched the hems of the leaden robes of cloud the sky had just doffed. Flocculent measures of vapor, like Golden Fleeces in an ethereal Pactolus; brilliant carmine and bronze patches struggling across the dome, catching the last reflections of the sun going down behind the Western ridges; amber-tinted zones, interspersed with steely-blue stripes resting upon the receding strata of snow clouds—were negligently mingled in a combination of rare beauty, in whose contemplation the weariness of official routine connected with the organization of a campaign was almost forgotten. The sharp boom of the evening gun signalled the descent of the Sun; slowly the golden tints of the cloud changed to bronze, to carmine, to a dull red; this latter turned into a pale amber blending imperceptibly into the darkness of night, relieved by myriads of sparkling stars. The atmosphere in its purity gave free passage to every beam of light, or reflected the slightest sounds. Only the crunching of feet trampling in the crisp, crystalline snow, or the barking of some shadow-scared hound, relieved the stillness. Night reigned supreme.[26]

Before long, sublime contemplation would give way to frenzied activity as Bourke and Smith, Dodge and Sergeant Major Walsh, Crook and companies prepared to splash across the icy North Platte toward the homes of the Northern Cheyennes.

And what of the Northern Cheyennes? How did they fare as the soldiers prepared to launch their invasion of the Powder River country? The Cheyennes had cherished few hopes since the June fight on the Little Bighorn River that white soldiers would leave

24. Ibid., Nov. 13, 1876.
25. Wheeler, *Frontier Trail*, 170–71.
26. Bourke diary, Nov. 11, 1876, 14:1383–84, He provided the same description in Bourke, *Mackenzie's Last*, 8.

them in peace. Immediately after that great victory, most of the Northern Cheyennes continued to travel with the Oglala Sioux, in part for protection. But after several weeks, the Cheyenne chiefs decided the moment had come to separate. Around the same time, a number of other Cheyennes, who had been living near Red Cloud Agency during the spring and summer, joined them. Government officials had been pressuring these people to unite with the Southern Cheyennes in Indian Territory. Concerned about the military campaigns being marshalled against their families and friends, and unwilling to acquiesce to demands that they give up the north country, they began moving north in July, in search of relatives. While an advance force of Colonel Wesley Merritt's Fifth Cavalry intercepted some of these Northern Cheyennes, Morning Star and his band successfully eluded the soldiers and hurried toward the Powder River country.[27]

By mid-November of that year, then, a large group of Northern Cheyennes had gathered to form a temporary village on the eastern flank of the Big Horn Mountains. Ever since Morning Star's band had joined the main body of Northern Cheyennes in July, three of the Old Man Chiefs had been present and the people felt heartened.[28] Furthermore, Coal Bear, Keeper of the Sacred Buffalo Hat, erected the Sacred Hat Tipi at each campsite, reminding all of the Hat's sacred presence and protective powers. In October the arrival of more bands from Red Cloud Agency, groups that slipped away when they became alarmed at the soldiers' warlike aspect, had augmented their numbers. Crook's and Mackenzie's movements to disarm and dismount Red Cloud's and Red Leaf's

---

27. See Thomas B. Marquis, *Wooden Leg: A Warrior Who Fought Custer*, 272–83; Powell, *People* 1:1048–49; and Powell, *Sweet Medicine* 1:126–28. Morning Star was born around 1808. He emerged as a leader of the Óhméséheso band in 1854, when he was 46 years old. As a young man he was notable as a brave warrior, and as he grew older his reputation as a wise person developed. In 1864, Morning Star was chosen for a second term as a chief because of his proven qualities of leadership, wisdom, and devotion to the Cheyenne sacred way of life. As the years went on, he became increasingly convinced that peace with the powerful whites offered the Cheyennes their only hope for survival, and so he was known as a peace chief. For more on Morning Star, see Powell, *People* 1:271, 377–78, 427–33, 453; and Grinnell, *Fighting Cheyennes*, 208–209, 234.

28. Wooden Leg said all four Old Man Chiefs were present at this time. See Marquis, *Wooden Leg*, 283.

bands confirmed their worst suspicions and heightened their sense of vulnerability. As a result, they had made their escape and found Morning Star's village in the mountains. Around the same time, Black Hairy Dog,[29] keeper of the Sacred Arrows, joined the camp and erected his lodge. Thus the Sacred Hat and Sacred Arrow Tipi were reunited, according to historian Peter Powell, their doorways facing the Sacred Mountain "from which flowed endless new life for the People."[30] Before November passed, the powers of the Hat and Arrows would be sorely tested by the soldiers and their Indian allies, who briefly passed on the banks of the North Platte River, before they began the march up the Bozeman Trail.

29. Black Hairy Dog succeeded his father, Stone Forehead, as keeper of the Sacred Arrows in 1876. He was born around 1823 and died in 1883. He was sent south after the Northern Cheyennes surrendered and remained there with the Sacred Arrows. See Powell, *People* 2:1162, 1418.

30. Ibid., 1050–51. See also Powell, *Sweet Medicine* 1:129–30.

CHAPTER 3

The March

The road to Fort Reno stretched toward the horizon, rambling over the low bluffs before the soldiers.[1] The intervening countryside between Forts Fetterman and Reno was not inviting to men more accustomed to eastern landscapes. It was a high, rolling mesa, fairly grassy, with occasional cottonwood trees clinging to the courses of insignificant streams—hardly worth the designation of waterways. The waters were brackish, and frequently vile. In the cold November morning light, the prospects of heading

1. Fort Reno was established June 28, 1866, about 1 mile north of the Fort Connor site. In 1865, Brig. Patrick E. Connor had established the latter post as a supply base for the 1865 Powder River Campaign. The next year, however, Col. Henry B. Carrington moved the post and renamed it in honor of Maj. Jesse L. Reno, killed in the Civil War. Fort Reno, built along the Powder River, was intended as protection for emigrants using the Bozeman Trail, but the army abandoned the post Aug. 18, 1868, as a result of the Fort Laramie Treaty of 1868. Indians burned it to the ground following its abandonment. In 1876, Capt. Edwin Pollock established Cantonment Reno 3 miles south of old Fort Reno as a supply base for military action in the Powder River Basin and as a demonstration of U.S. military power. The site was considered unhealthy, however, and on July 18, 1877, the post was moved to Clear Creek near present-day Buffalo, Wyo., and renamed Fort McKinney in honor of Lt. John A. McKinney, who died in the Dull Knife battle. See Frazer, *Forts*, 180–84. See also Murray, *Military Posts of Wyoming*, 55–57, and *Military Posts in the Powder River Country of Wyoming 1865–1894*, 13–27.

The *Harper's Weekly* view of *The Powder River Expedition Crossing the Platte,* published in December 1876. Credit: Wyoming State Archives, Museums and Historical Department

overland to the Powder River country could not have delighted many of the troopers.

One seasoned officer, however, awoke after a splendid night's rest on his trestle bed, eager to begin—as if off to sport, rather than war. Yet, even Lieutenant Colonel Richard Dodge understood that the first order of business—fording the North Platte River—held special perils for his infantrymen. "The river is my terror," he confided to his diary. While it was only about fifty yards wide near Fort Fetterman, the Platte was swift and full of floating ice on November 14, 1876. Furthermore, the banks were lined with ice several inches thick. Such conditions made crossing difficult, and Dodge was determined that none of his men would have to wade, although he noted that Mackenzie had no qualms about wetting the feet of his cavalrymen. To Colonel Dodge's great satisfaction, his men crossed over safely by 10:30 A.M. and began their march within the hour. But Mackenzie and the cavalry, he claimed, had a good start on them all.[2]

The expedition included eleven companies each of infantry and cavalry, four companies of artillery, about one hundred Pawnees, sixty Arapahoes, one hundred Sioux, a few Cheyennes, and a handful of white scouts. The Shoshone scouts would arrive en

2. See Dodge diary, Nov. 14, 1876, Newberry Library.

route to the battle. In addition, three hundred wagons, eight am-
bulances, and three hundred pack mules joined the column, carrying thirty days' worth of subsistence for the men and forage for
the horses and mules. Each company had two hundred rounds of
ammunition per man and the supply train carried at least three
hundred more. The army forces were great in number and heavily
armed. To Lieutenant Colonel Dodge it all made "a beautiful and
exhilarating [sic] sight—the long lines of Cavalry, Artillery, Infantry, Indians, pack mules and wagons. The ground was covered
with snow, but the day was perfectly lovely—too warm indeed
for good marching. The snow was in many places too deep and
wet for the Infantry to keep in—while the road was muddy and
slippery from the passage of so many animals and wagons."[3]

On horseback, Private Smith was spared the discomfort of a
muddy march, but his view of the first day out seems more pro-
saic than Dodge's—and certainly less enthusiastic:

Tuesday Nov. 14th 1876

It was very cold in the morning and the ice was flotting down the
river. We were all wadeing a round in the snow and [did] not now
[know] whether we were going to leave or not. Well a bout noon
we goot orders from genral Crook to pack up so we started and
marched 18 mils threw a worse cuntry than we had been in yet—
it was gitting from better to worse all the time. This Nite we
camped on Sage Brush Crick and there was nothing but sage Brush
to Birn.[4] It was hear that an Indin come in and gave the Genrol
[Mackenzie] an half of an antilope and the Gen. gave half of it to
us ordeles [orderlies] and that made us a good meal. We had more
to eate than if we had of been in our Company.[5]

---

3. Ibid., Nov. 14, 1876.

4. Lt. John Bourke noted in his diary that the infantry bivouaced 11 miles
out of Fort Fetterman on Sage Creek, but that the cavalry was obliged to march
an additional 4 miles to find other pools of brackish water in the same stream
bed. See Bourke diary, Nov. 14, 1876, microfilm copy, Denver Public Library,
1388. In his journal Lt. Col. Richard I. Dodge wrote: "I am camped at what is
called the 12 mile Camp on Sage Creek. The distance is really but little over 8
miles from Fort Fetterman, but all distances on the frontier are long when estimated by contractors who are paid by the 100 miles." See Dodge diary, Nov. 14,
1876, Newberry Library.

5. The basic field rations for campaigning soldiers consisted of salt pork,
hardtack, sugar, and coffee. For more information on this, see Don Rickey, Jr.,

Wensday Nov. 15 1876

Left camp as usual and made 15 mils and went in to camp on the South Fork of the Chyane [Cheyenne] River[6] and it was hear that the holl [whole] command camped to geather. We were well up in the Indine cuntry now and pooty wild to.

Thirsday Nov. 16 1876

Broke camp earley for we had to pool the wagons up a hill. This campe was in a kind of a bason [basin] and it was nice and warm and had lots of wood. The man that was cooking for the mes opend a can of lard and Gack Morrarity[7] the buglar went to work and cooked some Donuts and made some tea and this was the best supper I had on the trip. We pooled the wagons up the hill with roaps by hand.

Pleased with his doughnuts and antelope steak, Smith found the opening days of the Powder River Expedition went well. Other men, according to Sergeant James S. McClellan, of Company H, Third Cavalry, fared differently, for he noted that "Great numbers of the men have the diarrahea."[8] Even the initially ebullient Lieutenant Colonel Dodge began to exhibit moments of pique, particularly over issues of marching position, campsites, and leadership, as can be glimpsed in his diary entry for the day:

Nov. 16

Reveille at 5:15—broke camp 6:30. Moved to this early effort because General Crook gives his Indians [scouts] and pack mules

---

Forty Miles, 248–51. For information on daily rations for army regulars who were in garrison, see Coffman, *Old Army*, 340.

6. Dodge described this stream as "a miserable branch that can be stepped over anywhere." See Dodge diary, Nov. 15, 1876, Newberry Library.

7. This individual was not listed on the Field Staff and Band Muster Roll, Fourth Cavalry for Nov. 1876.

8. See Sgt. James S. McClellan Journal, Nov. 16, 1876, typescript copy loaned to author by Thomas R. Buecker, Fort Robinson Historic Site, Nebr., page 1. The original diary is available at the New York Public Library. McClellan's diary has been published several times. See Thomas R. Buecker, "The Journals of James S. McClellan," *Annals of Wyoming* 57 (Spring 1985), 21–34; James S. McClellan, "A Day With the 'Fighting Cheyennes': Stirring Scenes in the Old Northwest, Recalled for Motor Tourists," *Motor Travel Magazine* (Dec. 1930): 19–21; (Jan. 1931): 20–22; (Feb. 1931): 19–22; and Fred H. Werner, *The Dull Knife Battle*, 66–74.

the very best camps if they are ahead. Early as I was, however, McKenzie (sic) got ahead on the road with his wagons, I (from the peculiarly mean position assigned me last night) having to make over a mile of deep sand before I struck the road . . .

General Crook passes for a Sybarite—who utterly contems [sic] anything like luxury or even comfort—yet he has the most luxurious surroundings considering the necessity for short allowance that I have ever seen taken to the field by a General Officer. There is no doubt of his courage, energy, will—but I am loath to say I begin to believe he is a humbug—who hopes to make reputation by assuming qualities foreign to him. One thing is most certain. He is the very worst mannered man I have ever seen in his position. Though his ill manners seem to be the result rather of ignorance than of deliberate will. I believe him to be warm-hearted, but his estimate of a man will I think be discovered to be founded not on what that man can or will do for the service, but what he can or will do for Crook. It speaks badly for mankind when I am obliged to admit, that that kind are the successful men.

The day has been lovely. The silent shower of last night laid the dust and made marching good. Though McKenzie got his wagons first on the road I was a long way ahead of him with my troops and he was forced into all kinds of bad ground with his Command. I got to the camping place an hour ahead of my Command. Went to General Crook to see where I should camp, and was turned off to hunt for myself—all the choice spots being appropriated by him, his Indians, and pack mules. These two last are his hobbies and he rides them all the time—all the Headquarters animals, the pack mules and the mules of the supply trains are above us—while his Indians wash the entrails of the beeves in the stream from which his troops have to drink below. The Cavalry and Infantry are nobodies. The Indians and pack mules have all the good places. He scarcely treats McKenzie and I decently, but he will spend hours chatting pleasantly with an Indian or a dirty scout . . . I can't state what I see except in this private journal . . .

Went over at night to see McKenzie. He was most gentlemanly and agreeable and I enjoyed my visit. He gave me two orderlies, and asked me to call on him for any thing I want, and he would help me if he could . . . McKenzie and I agreed not to struggle for the road. He is to have it one day, I the next.

A blinding snowstorm ushered in the next morning, which, accompanied by a northwest wind, made riding and marching

miserable. His spirits renewed by the friendly chat with Colonel
Ranald Mackenzie, however, Dodge related the day's march with
characteristic aplomb and enthusiasm:

> ... For about an hour we had as lively a snow storm as I have seen
> ... the little hard pellets of snow striking the eyeballs were painful
> and tended to keep a man downcast. My men bore it bravely,
> though as the storm struck us after we broke camp many of them
> were without overcoats, and scarcely any had face protection. They
> plodded along, wind dead ahead blowing hard—cold as Christ-
> mas—without anything but their own stout hearts to protect
> them, and on a little let-up of the storm some glorious fellow
> struck up "We are marching on." At least a hundred voices joined
> in at once and though I was riding on the side of the column, have
> no more voice than a crow and moreover have the dignity of Act-
> ing Brigadier General to support, I could hardly refrain from strik-
> ing in.
>
> It is a glorious life, this soldiering. However great the trials,
> discomforts or suffering, there is pluck, endurance and patience to
> counterbalance all. We are going on a campaign fraught with not
> only the natural dangers from the enemy, but with a thousand
> unnamed dangers from the elements. Yet not a man flinches—not
> one but would rather suffer than turn back. A better Command
> than this never fell to the lot of a Commander and if Crook don't
> do something with it, he is a very unlucky, or incapable man.[9]

If Private Smith found soldiering "a glorious life" this day, he did
not say so. Nor did he mention any singing. In fact, his diary
entry was rather terse—a handful of words that speak volumes:

Friday Nov. 17 1876

Broke camp and marched 22 mils and camped on a unknown
crick.[10] It snod [snowed] all day and very cold.

Saturday Nov. 18 1876

We left camp at the usual time and after going a while the Gen
says Smith come with me. So him and me started out a hed on the

9. Dodge diary, Nov. 15, 1876, Newberry Library.
10. According to Bourke and Dodge, the column camped on the Dry Fork
of the Powder River on this night. See Dodge diary, Nov. 17, 1876, Newberry
Library, and Bourke diary, Nov. 17, 1876, Denver Public Library, 1389.

jump. We were going threw a nice valley[11] and we did not Stop till we goot in site of Fort Reno. So we went in and up to the Commanding officers [quarters] and found out where the best place to camp [was]. We went in to camp 1 mile below the Fort. This fort is bilt on a branch of the Podder [Powder] River and is bilt of logs. [There are] about 15 log cabins. That is all there is at this place and it is in site of the big horn Mountains. We had a hard time gitting the wagons a cross the crick. Had to pull them across with ropes.[12]

Our camp was a nice camp. There was a big bank on the North of us and that kept the wind off it [the camp]. It was hear that we cut our first cotnwood to feed our horses in stid of hay. This kind of work lasted till we goot back [from the campaign]. It was a grate bother.

The fort, or more accurately, Cantonment Reno, had been established earlier that year to serve as a supply base for expeditions staying out in the field during the winter and as a major demonstration of military presence in that country. It was situated on the west bank of the Powder River, about three miles upstream from the original Fort Reno, established in 1865 and abandoned in 1868. Colonel Dodge did not conceal his disappointment in the Powder River, the cantonment, or the post infantry commander. Of the river, he complained, "instead of the clear sparkling stream I expected to find, it is a murky, dis-colored pea soup kind of a stream, almost as filthy as the Missouri itself." Of the fort, he wrote: "It is a horrible place to be confined at all winter, and I had rather take my chances of our Indian bullets, of freezing or starvation for six weeks, than to have to stay here till spring." About Captain Edwin Pollock,[13] who commanded the garrison's four companies of infantry, Colonel Dodge concluded: "Pollock is

11. This would be the valley created by the Dry Fork of the Powder River.

12. Dodge reported this difficulty in his journal: "Many of McKenzie's teams were stuck in the ford and he came near losing some animals. Profiting by his experience, all my wagons got over safely." Dodge diary, Nov. 18, 1876, Newberry Library.

13. Captain Pollock, hailing from Pennsylvania, originally joined the military during the Civil War, when he enlisted as a private in the 25th Pennsylvania Infantry. In 1864, Pollock became a captain, and he remained in that rank until his retirement in Feb. 1885. See Heitman, *Historical Register*, 796.

Old Fort Reno, from the South—Now Depot of Supplies for General Crook, drawn for *Harper's Weekly* and published in December 1876. Credit: Wyoming State Archives, Museums and Historical Department

the most conceited ass that ever existed. He thinks he can give advice to the Almighty, and talks to General Crook and everybody else as if he tolerated them. He is only a fair officer, scarcely above the average as a worker and very much below it as a man of sense and discretion. He always disgusts me, and he did it tonight. How he manages to hoodwink such men as Crook and Sheridan can only be explained on the principle that he who blows loudest will always find some one to listen." [14]

Lieutenant John Bourke, whose diary lacks the vim and vinegar of Dodge's, exhibited more charity toward Pollock, praising his energy and efficiency in administering the construction activities of the cantonment. He also, as Crook's aide, was privy to events that neither Dodge nor Private Smith knew about. That evening, for example, he reported in his journal that six Arapahoes and eight Sioux, with four days' rations, left Reno to scout along and across the Big Horn Mountains. [15] He also indicated that the paymaster had arrived—news that especially interested young Smith:

14. Dodge diary, Nov. 18, 1876, Newberry Library.
15. Bourke diary, Nov. 18, 1876. Denver Public Library, 1390–91. Sioux interpreter Billy Garnett testified, years later, that 5 Arapahoes and 5 Sioux left Cantonment Reno that evening. See "Survey Notes, William Garnett at Cane Creek, S.D., 1907," Eli Seavey Ricker Collection, Nebraska State Historical Society, Box 4, Tablet 1, 107.

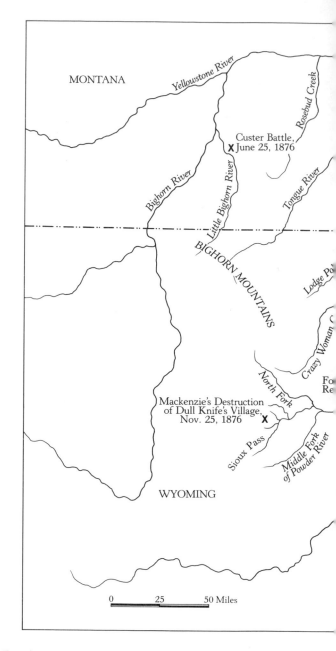

MONTANA

Yellowstone River

Rosebud Creek

Custer Battle,
X June 25, 1876

Bighorn River

Little Bighorn River

Tongue River

BIGHORN MOUNTAINS

Lodge Po

Crazy Woman C

North Fork

Fo
Re

Mackenzie's Destruction
of Dull Knife's Village,
Nov. 25, 1876 **X**

Sioux Pass

Middle Fork
of Powder River

WYOMING

0   25   50 Miles

Powder River Expedition

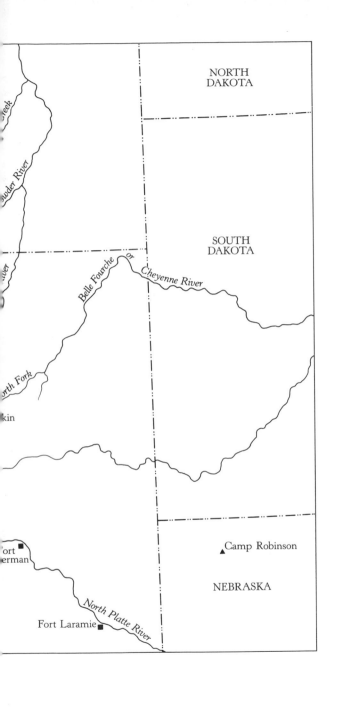

Sunday Nov. 19 1876

We lay over hear all day and goot Pade [paid].[16] This was the first
pay day I ever poot any money a way with the Pay master. I poot
18 dollars with him to start with. I dont supose I would of done
this only I had mad[e] a strong resilution never to tutch whiskey a
gane.

Well us boys thought we had to have some thing better to eate
so we throde in and made up a nuff to bye a lot of cand stuff sutch
as corn and tomatoes. Well we did a feast while this stuff lasted.
And hear I had a fus with the Sadler Sargant—a little dride up fist
but I dare not tell him this. He went to the Gen about me and the
Gen cold me up and told me he did not want to realeve me and if
I had any thing to complane about to come to him and this settled
it all.

We wound up the day by cutting cotton wood. There were a
grate menney drunk to nite.[17]

November 19 was notable not only for the paymaster's presence
and the ensuing debauchery but also for a more solemn occasion—a meeting between Indian scouts from eight tribes and
General Crook.[18] Fortunately, Lieutenant Bourke attempted a record of the scouts' comments, although, as Colonel Dodge noted
in his account, the lines of communication were muddled at best.

16. Enlisted men were paid between $13 (for a private) and $34 a month (for
an ordnance sergeant). After 1872, Congress instituted longevity increases
amounting to $1 more per month in the third year of service, $2 in the fourth
year, and $3 in the fifth year. All longevity pay was retained until the soldier
was discharged, at a 4 percent interest rate. Soldiers were paid at lengthy intervals, and soon after they received it, they often spent their pay at the post trader's
or sutler's store. Having the paymaster hold some pay was like starting a savings
account. See Rickey, Forty Miles, 126–29; Coffman, Old Army, 349–50.

17. Of all this Dodge noted in his diary: "We have no end of trouble today
with drunken men and tonight three shots have been fired in camp. I asked
General Crook to shut up the Trading Store, but he being a personal friend (it
is said they are partners in a sheep ranch in Oregon) of the trader, refused, and
said I could regulate it. So I could so far as my own command is concerned, but
I had no right to regulate Cavalry, teamsters, and others not of my Command,
so after standing it as long as I could, I wrote a note to Pollock, Commanding
Post, and asked him to shut it—which he did." See Dodge diary, Nov. 19, 1876,
Newberry Library.

18. Bourke listed the 8 tribes as Sioux, Cheyennes, Arapahoes, Pawnees,
Shoshones, Utes, Bannocks, and Nez Perces. See Bourke diary, Nov. 10, 1876,
Denver Public Library, 1391.

The Arapahoe Sharp Nose's speech, for example, was interpreted from Arapahoe to Sioux to English to other tribal languages for the benefit of the rest of the Indian participants. "Anyone who has ever played the old game of story telling, where each player hears the whispered story from his neighbor on one side and whispers it to his neighbor on the other side," Dodge wryly noted, "can imagine what the speech must have been when filtered through so many ... In such a Babel of language it is only a wonder how any one could understand."[19] Flawed as the interpretations probably were, they nevertheless provide the best record of scouts' viewpoints available from the Powder River Expedition's written documents, and so merit some attention.

Crook's purpose was to set down some ground rules for the coming conflict. The crusty West Pointer cautioned the Indian auxiliaries against killing women and children (an order, as events will prove, Anglo-American soldiers needed to hear too)— arguing, for reasons not so much of humanity but strategy, for capturing and using them as hostages to lure in the men. "We don't want to kill the Indians," Crook claimed, "we only want to make them behave themselves. We want to find the village and make the Indians give up their ponies & guns, so that in future they will have to behave themselves."[20] In addition, he implored these Indians to put aside past differences and remain friends through the course of the campaign, to avoid wasting ammunition, to refrain from allowing the enemy to escape in their enthusiasm to capture stock, and to agree that Crook would divide all plunder taken in a fight among the various tribes, as a means to reduce the potential for quarreling.

What these Indian participants thought of Crook's remarks, Bourke's account does not say. They were, however, apparently concerned about getting along with one another on the expedition and about appeasing Crook to insure peace for their families in the future. Sharp Nose, an Arapaho, spoke first:

I have waited a long time to meet all these people and make peace.
We have been living a long time with the white man and follow

19. Dodge diary, Nov. 19, 1876, Newberry Library.
20. Quoted in Bourke diary, Nov. 19, 1876, Denver Public Library, 1392–93.

the white man's road and do what he says. I hope these people [other Indians present] will do the same. We have all met here today to make peace and I hope we'll remain at peace. And I hope General Crook will take pity on us and help us. . . . I hold my hand up to the Great Spirit and swear I'll stick to General Crook as long as I'm with him. When this war is over and I get home, I want to live like a white man and have implements to work with. We have made peace with these people here today and we'd like to have a letter sent home to let our people know about it.[21]

Li-Heris-oo-la-shar, a Pawnee also known as Frank White or Leading Chief, spoke next.[22] Like most of the others, he wore a military uniform, but his painted face, head, and ears lent an ex-

21. Ibid., 1393–94.

22. Several different participants in this campaign left descriptions of Li-Heris-oo-la-shar, including Bourke, who said that he "had a good face, prominent cheek bones, acquiline nose, large mouth and frank, open eyes, not so piercing as those usually to be noticed among the aborigines. He had the air of a far-seeing, judicious law-giver, one who took note of all he saw and whose advice could be relied on. Yet, he was no lamb, as the outlines of his countenance plainly showed that, if aroused, he would be a bad enemy." See Bourke, *Mackenzie's Last*, 14. Providing a different view, Frank North commented: "Capt. Bourke's narrative of the Dull Knife fight gives a very entertaining sketch of Li-Heris-oo-la-shar's conspicuous participation in the 'great talk' held near Cantonment Reno on the way up to the Big Horn Mountains, how he was dressed on that occasion, and the Pawnee sergeant's desire to be known and considered as a white man. Though not really a chief, he was a man of force and character; and many anecdotes—probably some traditional—have been handed down about him." By describing Bourke's account as "entertaining," North may be suggesting that the lieutenant embellished a bit and, also, that Li-Heris-oo-la-shar's comments during the council did not necessarily represent the feelings of all the Pawnee present. See Captain L. H. North, "The Fighting Norths and Pawnee Scouts," *Motor Travel Magazine* (March 1931): 21. On another occasion North described the Pawnee scout as "not only a warrior but something of an orator and man of affairs—what might be called a progressive Indian, who could take care of himself on almost any occasion." See North, *Man of the Plains*, 233–34. It should come as no surprise that Lt. Col. Dodge found this Pawnee attractive. Dodge and Li-Heris-oo-la-shar had actually met before this 1876 Campaign: "My old friend Frank White made an excellent speech. This is the man, with whom I was cornered by about 45 Sioux on the Loup in 1867. . . . He is a gallant fellow and steadfast friend and I am glad to find that he is now Head Chief of the Pawnees" (Dodge diary, Nov. 19, 1876, Newberry Library). As North noted, however, White was not "Head Chief." He lived well into the twentieth century, long enough to see Indian Territory become the state of Oklahoma (North, "The Fighting Norths," 21).

otic air to his appearance. After glancing toward the heavens, Li-
Heris-oo-la-shar spoke:

I am talking to friends. This is our head chief (General Crook)
talking to us and asking us to be brothers. I hope the Great Spirit
will smile on us. Brothers. We are all Indians and have all the same
kind of skin. The Pawnees have lived with the white men a long
time and know how strong they are. We are afraid of them, because they are so strong. Brothers. I don't think there is one of you
can come out here today and say you have ever heard of the Pawnee killing a white man. Brothers. We are all of the same color and
we are all Indians. Today, this Big Chief has called us together to
have a Council and I am glad of it and glad to meet you all. Father,
(turning to General Crook), I suppose you know the Pawnees are
civilized. We plough, farm and work the ground like white people.
Father, it is so what the Arapahoes said. We have all gone on this
Expedition to help you and hope it may be a successful one.

Father, I'm glad you have said you would listen to what we had
to say. If we have any wrongs, we'll come to you to tell about them.
I suppose you have heard it is a good many years since we (Pawnees) have been to war. We have given it up long ago. When I was
at home, I did what our Agent wanted us to do: farmed and
worked the land. When they said at Washington, they wanted us
for this trip, we threw everything aside but when we go back, we'll
take to farming again. Father, it is good what you have said to us.
I hope these people understand it too and that we shall all be good
friends. This is all I have to say. I am glad you have told us what
you did about the captured stock. The horses taken will help us to
work our land.[23]

After several more speeches there were handshakes and promises of friendship all around. Interpreter Billy Garnett later remembered that the meeting had an exceedingly conciliatory effect
on all. Up to this time, the Sioux had been rather reserved toward
the other Indians and the Pawnees had been especially suspicious
of the Sioux. Now, however, these former enemies became allies.[24]

While the Indian auxiliaries and officers made their peace, the
whiskey trader made his profits. The effects of the latter, however,
were not nearly as salubrious. The pedlar's cart was confiscated

23. Quoted in Bourke diary, November 19, 1876, Denver Public Library,
1396.
24. "Survey Notes," Tablet 1, 72–73.

and the barrels knocked in, yet not before many men had tasted his wares and tragedy had struck. If Private Smith was privy to the Indian council, he did not mention it. He did know about the whiskey and the ensuing troubles:

Monday Nov. 20th 1876

Lade over today, all day, and run a round with orders. Last nite while one of the boys belonging to the 5 Cavelery was on a drunk he goot so drunk that he fell in to the crick and goot wet and lad out on the bank. He frose to death and his company planted him in the after noon.[25]

I was up with the Gen. to the Post and goot my supper with the company there. There were a grate menney drunk up there to day.

Tuesday Nov. 21 1876

We broke camp and moved camp about 2 mils up the crick. It was hear I was poot in to cook for they thought it was my turn.[26] Well, I was satsfide and went at it and the first thing I done was to bake bred and I burnt up the first pan. I finley mad[e] a pooty good cook out of my self. And now it was that they all let up on that handy name Smith. They had near wore it out. I had fool swing now to do as I pleased. The onely thing that botherd me the first day was to carred [carry] wotter about half a mile in camp kittles. It was a very slopy day.

Wensday Nov. 22nd 1876

Left camp at Seven oclock and made 28 mils and camped on Crazy Woman's fork. It was the day that the Grate Sargent Mager [Walsh] begon to think there was a going to bee a fite soon and he

25. Lt. Bourke corroborated Smith's account concerning the dead soldier. See Bourke diary, Nov. 20, 1876, Denver Public Library, 1401–1402, and Bourke, *Mackenzie's Last*, 12–13. Sgt. McClellan noted in his diary, however, that 2 men died—one from Company H, 5th Cavalry, and one from the artillery. He did not explain the causes of death. See McClellan diary, author's copy, 2. Lt. Col. Dodge made no mention of any deaths in his journal. He did indicate, though, that officers too had enjoyed a drink or two the previous night: "After I had written up my Diary last night, and was comfortably in bed, two red-legged beauties, [J. B.] Campbell and [Frank G.] Smith, came in and chinned me for an hour, and drank up nearly a bottle of my whiskey (with a little help from me)." See Dodge diary, Nov. 20, 1876, Newberry Library.

26. According to Edward Coffman, cooks were detailed for 10 days at a time and received no extra compensation for their work. Cooking was hard work and not a favored chore. Coffman, *Old Army*, 342.

got the roomitise [rheumatism] all at once and could not wride his horse and had to ride in the amblance. I was glad to git rid of him, for I hatted [hated] him worse than a snake. This was a very cold day.

Thursday Nov. 23rd 1876

This morning a bout sun up we saw an Indin comming in with two ponies and carring a white flag. He come up to our Gen. and shook hands and it turned out to be two Bors [Sitting Bear][27] that the Gen. had sent out from Red Cloud [Agency] to hunt an I [Indian] camp and to meet us hear. He had been out now 1 month. Then he and our Genral went up to Genral Crooks quarters and they had a big pow wow. The Indin sed there was a camp 45 mils to the north and he had been in the camp.[28] Then Gen. Crook gave our Gen. orders to take all the Cavelery and all the Indins and the pack trane with 10 days raishons and go and try and bring them in and not to have a fite if he could avoid it and this Indin two Bors [Sitting Bear] would be our guide. The Genril come back to our quarters and told us to pack our three meals as quick as we could and bee reddy to start and all the companys goot orders to the same affect. I had it a little better here a gane than if I had of been in my company for I was alode [allowed] to put all my blankets on the muls and the boys in the company could only carrey one and that on there hors. And we had all we wanted to eate on our muls. Well about noon we left and made 11 mils and camped on an annone [unknown] Crick.[29] We left the wagon trane correld with the Infraty with it and more men with poor horses. Very cold today.

Reconnaissance of Sioux and Cheyenne positions had indeed brought valuable information. Even before Sitting Bear's arrival, the Sioux and Arapahoe scouts sent out from Cantonment Reno

27. Although Smith identified this man as Two Bears, he was actually known to the whites on the expedition as Sitting Bear. Bourke and Garnett said he was Cheyenne. Garnett noted that Sitting Bear had a family back at Red Cloud Agency. He added the Indians at that agency were suspicious of him, especially the Cheyennes who were with the Sioux, and denounced him as a "spotter," advising he be cast out or killed. He at last made up his mind to get away from these Cheyennes and went to work for Crook. See "Survey Notes," Tablet 1, 120–22.

28. This would be Morning Star's Northern Cheyenne village.

29. McClellan identified this as a creek that emptied into Crazy Woman Creek. See McClellan Journal, Nov. 23, 1876, author's copy, 2.

had returned with a prize captive—the young Northern Cheyenne Many Beaver Dams—who had been drawn to their bivouac near Clear Creek by their campfires.[30] The Arapahoe scouts and Red Shirt, a Sioux, all excellent sign-talkers, engaged the young Cheyenne in conversation while he ate at the Arapahoe fire. As they had hoped, Many Beaver Dams related the location and size of various Sioux and Northern Cheyenne villages. Only when he had finished, did the Arapahoes brandish their revolvers and reveal their true purpose.[31] On November 21 they brought their captive back to Cantonment Reno where Crook interrogated him. At that point, the general dashed off a telegram to Sheridan: "Scouts returned and reported that the Cheyennes have crossed over to the other [east] side of the Big Horn Mountains and that Crazy Horse and his band are encamped on the Rosebud near where we said [sic] the fight with them last June. We start out after his band tomorrow morning."[32]

Crook's plan to push out from Crazy Woman's Creek and strike Crazy Horse's village changed, however, when Sitting Bear arrived with the news that Many Beaver Dams' small village had taken alarm and had moved to join, and warn, Crazy Horse of the troops' presence. This scout also reported that an extremely large Cheyenne village was situated in the Big Horn Mountains.[33] Crook ordered Colonel Ranald Mackenzie and most of the cavalry and Indian auxiliaries to move up Crazy Woman's Fork in order to surprise and destroy the Northern Cheyenne village and compel its occupants' surrender. Accordingly, a very small detachment of Indian scouts, selected for their knowledge of the country and good judgment, preceded the main body of soldiers.[34] Colonel

30. Garnett listed the 5 Sioux scouts involved in this mission as Red Shirt, Six Feather, Little Bull, White Face, and Red Horse. Garnett added: "Every step from Fort Robinson to Reno Old Sitting Bull and Crazy Horse and all the holdout Indians knew what Indians Crook had taken with him as scouts, and who the chief scouts were." This comment suggests the gravity involved in scouting against one's fellow Sioux. See "Survey Notes," Tablet 1, 107.
31. Ibid., 110–14.
32. Crook to Philip Sheridan, Nov. 23, 1876, Box 17, "Sioux War" Special File, Division of the Missouri, RG 393, NARS.
33. "Survey Notes," Tablet 1, 123.
34. Garnett identified Sharp Nose as the guide leading the whole command. Kills a Hundred (later known as Red Dog), Little Battle, and Skunk Head were

Richard Dodge and his infantry, as Private Smith noted, remained behind, as did General Crook. When the doughboys received word that they were to unpack their wagons and pitch their tents—when they realized the fight would be left to the horse-men—they were, according to Dodge, "quite delighted and yelled lustily." As for Dodge, the officer hoped "with all [his] heart" that Mackenzie would be successful and settled down to read *Jane Eyre*, play whist, and await the cavalry's return.[35]

This march from Crazy Woman Creek into the Big Horn Mountains was fraught with excitement, tension, and certainly, anxiety. It also became a very difficult march, according to Bourke. With his flair for the dramatic, he claimed the "grim bosom of the Big Horn Mountains parted to admit the column into a deep canon whose vertical walls carved into turrets and battlements by the erosion of time and the elements, proclaimed . . . almost with the eloquence of human tongue that those who entered must leave all hope behind."[36] As the troopers floundered, slipped, and struggled over smooth rock, they remained (for the most part) silent, kept close when possible, and occasionally smoked—although they had orders to refrain. A few of the sol-diers and scouts took sick, perhaps from the altitude, cold tem-peratures, and fear.[37] Among them rode Private Smith, who as-sumed his position with the column. He describes these events:

Friday Nov. 24th 1876

Left camp 8 oclock. Since we left the wagon trane I had to stay with the Pack trane to look out for our muls for I was cook. We marched 10 mils and hear we met an Indin [scout] and he told us we were close on to an Indin [Northern Cheyenne] camp. So we made a holt [halt] right at the foot of the Big horn mountains and it was a nice place to. We were not a loud to bild any firs an so we

---

among the Sioux in this small detachment of scouts at the head of the troops. See Garnett, "Survey Notes," Tablet 1, 124–25. See also Bourke, *Mackenzie's Last*, 15–16.

35. Dodge diary, Nov. 23, 1876, Newberry Library.

36. Bourke, *Mackenzie's Last*, 24.

37. See Bourke diary, Nov. 23, 1876, Denver Public Library, 1411–14, and North, *Man of the Plains*, 211–12. See also, Bourke, *Mackenzie's Last*, 22–24, and McClellan Journal, author's copy, 2–3.

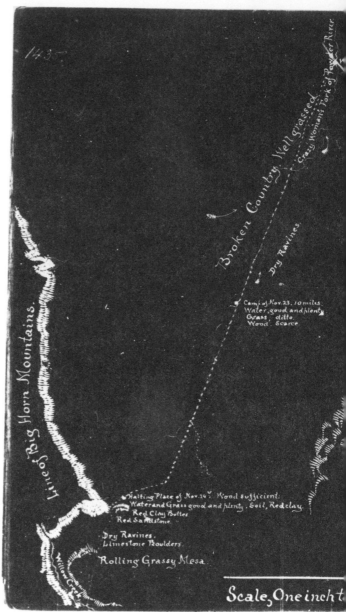

Lieutenant John Bourke's drawings of the cavalry's march to the village site and the battlefield. Credit: Western History Department, Denver Public Library (microfilm). The original Bourke diary is held at the United States Military Academy Library, Special Collections Division.

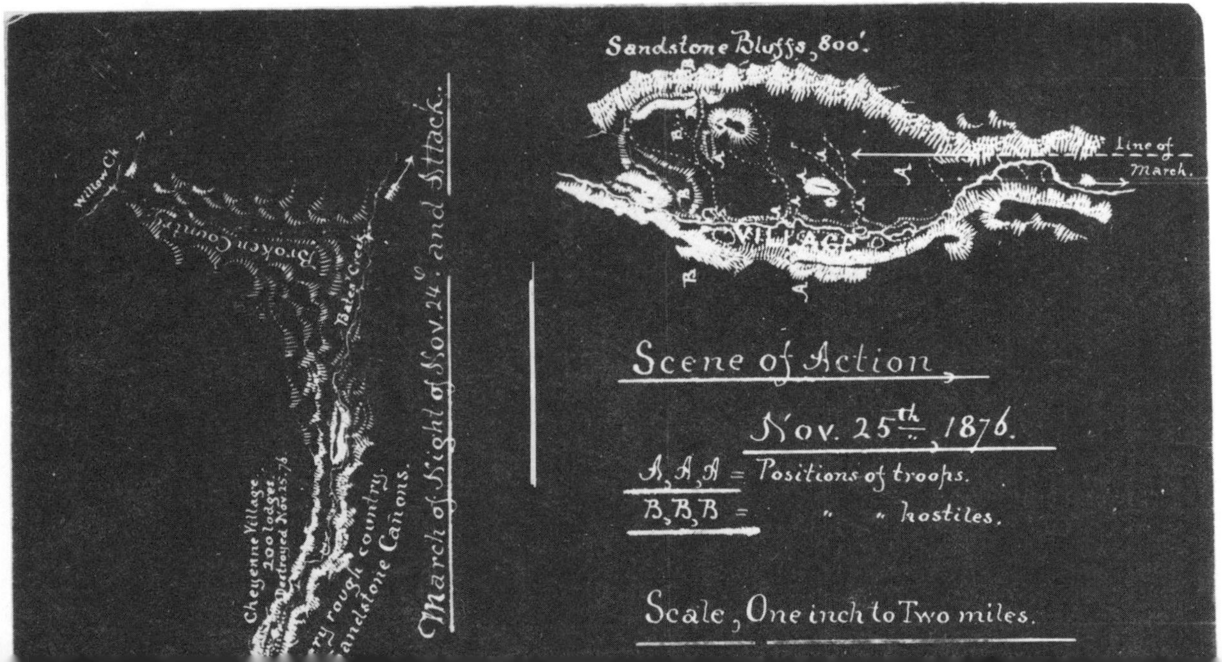
Willow Ck
Broken Country
Bates' Creek
Cheyenne Village
200 lodges
Destroyed Nov. 25. 76.
ry rough country
andstone Cañons.
March of Night of Nov. 24th and Attack.
Sandstone Bluffs, 800'.
VILLAGE
Line of March.
Scene of Action
Nov. 25th, 1876.
A, A, A = Positions of troops.
B, B, B = " " hostiles.
Scale, One inch to Two miles.

had to eate our raishons—raw fat pork and hard tack. We lay still till nite and nobody was a loud on any of the hills around. We had not been hear long when a soldier came dashing in to camp and sed they were a comming. Well that cosd [caused] quite a stampeed amung the men and we all started for our horses in the hird but it was nothing but some of our Indins looking a round for Signs [of the enemy]. You can see now that they ought not to inlist boys to send out to fite Indins. They air [are] not the thing a toll in this cuntry. They air to frade [afraid] and [ought] not to be on Post. I will keep on till 12 oclock at nite.

Lieutenant Bourke had also noted the arrival of the Indian scouts and the flurry of rumors that swept the ranks at their approach. Under the circumstances of such a march, he explained in his diary, "all kinds of rumors spontaneously germinate: everybody has his own story and while anxious to impart it to all about him, is equally anxious to hear and adopt their rumors."[38] After boiling down all reports, Mackenzie learned the main village had been located not far from the troopers' present position, which was at the base of the Big Horn Mountains. He ordered the men to remain under cover of a projecting ledge of rocks. Just before dark, they began crawling through a narrow ravine, forging ahead to their deadly destination.[39] Private Smith, however, received word that he was to remain behind:

About sun down we goot orders to saddle up and have every thing straped tite. I now found that I was to bee left with the pack muls, but I could not stand that a toll so I went to the Genrall and told him that I wanted to go a long with him for I wanted to see all the sits [sights] there was to bee seen. So he told me I could and left another ordly with the mules. We started out and climed the first hill on our right and I dont [k]now how we ever goot up and this kind of marching lasted all nite. A grate many horses gave out and some could not clime the mountains. The Indines now began to pass us one and two at a time till they all goot by us. We were not aloud to speak or lite a match. In some places we had to go in single file and that strung the colm [column] out five or six mils. If the hostils had of none [known] we were a comming they could

38. Bourke diary, Nov. 24, 1876, Denver Public Library, 1411.
39. Ibid., 1412.

of cild [killed] every man of us in some of these places. Well about 2 o'clock we came into a nice valey. They call it Sioux Pass.[40] It was the nisest place I ever saw. About five mils long and on one side there was a wall of stone just as thoe it had of been bilt and on the other side there was mountains and they were coverd with fine treas. And it was about one hundred yards wide and the moon shone in at one end and it was a splend[id] site to see the boddy of horses mooving along and not a sound to bee hird as the ground was like a carpet. I believe the wall of rocks stood one thousand feet high.

Well when we came to the end of this pass we found the Indins all unsaddling and saddling their war ponies, gitting reddy for war and they changed their close [clothes] and got on their war dres and painted themselves up.[41] and they did look wild anuff. Some did look hiddeous. We mad[e] a halt hear for 10 or 15 minutes and the Indin sed we were near the camp. We started ahed and past the Indins hear [auxiliaries] and marched over a worse cuntry than we had been in before as we were going up a affle big mountane. We hird a shot a way in the rear. Then you had out [ought] to hear the Genrall curse. He was to mad for any youse.[42] We found out after wards it was a man shot his plade [played] out horse. When we goot to the top of the mountane we made a halt for there had

40. Lieutenant Bourke was also struck with the beauty of this place: "We were in a 'pass' in the Big Horn Mountains, high walls of earth and rocks on both sides, with trees thickly congregated together near the crest, while our trail ran along a perfectly smooth causeway of velvet grass. This place has been aptly named by the Sioux 'the race-course.'" Bourke diary, Nov. 24, 1876, Denver Public Library, 1414.

41. Col. Homer Wheeler claimed that the Pawnee scouts stripped to G-strings, removed their heavy boots for moccasins, and tied handkerchiefs around their heads so that they could be distinguished from the hostiles. This was typical battle attire for Pawnees. See Buecker and Paul, "The Pawnee Scouts," 17.

42. At one point, according to Bourke, the column was delayed 1 hour and, at another point, 2 hours—delays that annoyed Col. Mackenzie. In addition, his "natural impatience was aggravated by the solicitude of our Indian guides, who kept coming back every few moments to urge the column forward, saying in a low tone to the interpreters that the hostile village was at hand." Bourke believed the Indian scouts revealed much greater anxiety than the white soldiers, perhaps because they better understood the gravity of the situation. All understood, however, that not a moment was to be wasted if the element of surprise was to be maintained and the loss of life, on the troops' side, was to be minimized. Bourke diary, Nov. 24, 1876, 1415; Bourke, *Mackenzie's Last*, 24–25.

not [been] any Indins come ahed since we had mad[e] the last halt.
And I thought the Genrall thought we were being drawd in to a
trap and he mad[e] all the Indins march ahed.

Well we went down off of the mountane and went about 2 mils
and the Gude [guide] says stop and come with me. We halted and
the Gen. went ahead with the Indin and in about 10 or 15 minutes
he come back and sed tighteng your saddels and git reddy for a
charge. It was now just dawn of day and [I] could jest see a little.
The Generall now went back and told all the companys to git
reddy for a dash for it was to late to surround the camp but not to
shoot unless they shot first. The Gen. come a hed now and I hird
the Generall tell Leut. Leatton [Lawton] how we would have to do
it. He sed we were to late to surround the camp and we would have
to make a dash for it. He says we will keep the Indins [auxiliaries]
right a hed of us and make them go in first and if there is any trap,
they will catch it first and then we can open on them from the
rear. It was now I thought of [the] Custer Mascree and began to
think what I was about to go into. . . .

What Private Smith did not mention was the sound of Cheyenne drumming emanating from the village—something that had
caught the ear of Lieutenant Bourke: " . . . we soon heard in a
vague but awe-inspiring sort of indistinctness the thump! thump!
of war drums, and the jingling of their rattles sounding the measure of a war-dance."[43] As scouts and soldiers prepared to charge,
however, the drumming had stopped. The Northern Cheyennes
had gone to bed after a long winter's night of dance.

Morning Star's village rested in a fortresslike park where the Red
Fork of the Powder River made its way through the Big Horn
Mountains. The spot offered much protection, for it had few en-
trances and its surface undulated with bluffs, hills, and ridges.
Occasional runs and coulees sliced the valley where the Red Fork,
at least on warmer days, flowed through its center. On this day,
the Northern Cheyennes' lodges huddled near the stream, which

43. Bourke diary, Nov. 24, 1876, Denver Public Library, 1415. Garnett remembered these sounds too: "Indian scouts were chafing to spring on the village
as daylight was breaking and they could hear the strains of music and other
sounds of merriment and knew that the village was all unconscious of the presence of any foe." See "Survey Notes," Tablet 1, 137–38.

was lined with cottonwood, box elder, and willow. The trees afforded further protection by screening the homes from an intruder's view until he was nearly upon them. This was a site clearly chosen for its defensive as well as aesthetic aspects. Yet at dawn on November 25, 1876, all of its natural advantages would not deter the United States Army.

It was five months, to the day, since the Northern Cheyennes' stunning victory over the white men at the Little Bighorn. They certainly knew that white soldiers were combing the countryside and that they were the quarry. Most probably were not surprised when, on November 21, some hunters arrived in the village with news of tracks from many horses. On the next day the Council Chiefs dispatched four scouts, or "wolves," to learn more. Hail, Crow Necklace, Two Moon, and High Wolf saddled their horses and set out on their reconnaissance mission.[44]

On November 23 they discovered the huge army camp on Crazy Woman Creek and the presence of Indian soldier-scouts as well. Lying flat on a hill above the enormous camp, they watched all day. After nightfall, Two Moon and Crow Necklace cut loose three horses near the Pawnee camp and spirited away their prizes. In the meantime, Hail and High Wolf had fallen asleep. The horses in their keep, of course, had wandered away. Undaunted, the four men galloped off on their new horses, soon overtook their own, and headed back to Morning Star's village, which in their absence, had moved to the protected spot on the Red Fork.[45]

The four scouts reported their news about the presence of white and Indian enemies nearby and predicted that, if these soldiers reached Morning Star's village, a big fight would follow. Little Wolf, Morning Star, and Old Bear (the three Old Man Chiefs present), Black Hairy Dog (keeper of the Sacred Arrows) and Coal Bear (keeper of the Sacred Hat) all listened carefully, as did those members of the council of Forty-four who were on hand. Black Hairy Dog spoke first and urged his people to move immediately and join a large Oglala village not far away.[46] Besides

44. Grinnell, *Fighting Cheyennes*, 370.
45. Ibid., 373. See also Stands in Timber, *Cheyenne Memories*, 214–15.
46. Grinnell, *Fighting Cheyennes*, 374; Powell, *People* 2:1054.

the wolves' report, the Cheyennes had Box Elder's vision to consider. Earlier that morning, Box Elder, an eighty-year-old, blind medicine man noted for his gift of prophecy, had dreamed that soldiers and enemy scouts attacked the village from the east, killing some of the Cheyennes.[47] All signs, sacred and otherwise, indicated that flight was the wisest option open to them.

Acting in defiance of both Black Hairy Dog's counsel and Box Elder's vision, however, Last Bull—head chief of the Kit Fox military society—stepped forward and announced that the Northern Cheyennes would stay and fight. Furthermore, all would join in a celebration of the Kit Foxes' recent victory over a party of Shoshones by attending a campfire and dancing in their honor that evening. If soldiers attacked, they would be awake and ready to repel them. When some people prepared to move away, Last Bull and other Kit Fox society members stopped them. Not one of the Council Chiefs, not one of the Old Man Chiefs resisted Last Bull's order.[48]

His order, in the end, proved a fatal mistake. What possessed this man to ignore the intelligence of the wolves and the sacred power of Box Elder's vision? Why did he insist on a dance instead of defense, particularly the kind of defensive action that might have spelled victory for the Northern Cheyennes had they posted scouts along the narrow entrance to the valley, which had struck both Private Smith and Colonel Mackenzie as a perfect place for

47. Stands in Timber, *Cheyenne Memories*, 214; Powell, *Sweet Medicine* 1:154–55; and Powell, *People* 2:1056. Box Elder was also known as Brave Wolf, Maple, Maple Tree, Dog on the Range, Dog Standing, and Dog on the Ridge. He was the son of a holy man named Horn or Old Horn. His own reputation grew after he led a charge against Crows and Shoshones in 1830 under the protection of a sacred whistle his father gave him. Horn eventually instructed Box Elder in his own sacred knowledge. He was a humble man, always traveling on foot. Box Elder traveled at night, entering a village late. But people always knew when he was coming for they heard his sacred whistle. His father also gave him the Sacred Wheel Lance, which had the power to throw a mantle of invisibility over whoever carried it. For more on Box Elder and his role in Northern Cheyenne history, see Powell, *People* 1:16–18, 188, 271, and 2:758, 792–93, 816–17, 820, 824, 934, 937, 1126, and 1419.

48. Stands in Timber, *Cheyenne Memories*, 216; Powell, *People*, 2:1054; and Grinnell, *Fighting Cheyennes*, 369.

ambush? The answers to these questions come down to matters of personality, power, and pride. By 1876 many Northern Cheyennes increasingly perceived Last Bull and the Kit Fox society as not only arrogant but even overbearing. They called them "Wife Stealers" and "Beating-up Soldiers" and were contemptuous yet afraid of them too. Simultaneously, regard for the Elk Scrapers, a rival military society, grew, as did their reputations for leadership. By 1876 three of the four Old Man Chiefs belonged to the esteemed Elk Scrapers society.[49]

The rivalry between the Kit Foxes and Elk Scrapers had been keen during the previous February when Last Bull warned a Cheyenne village about nearby soldiers. The Elks ignored, even snubbed him, but similar warnings from others were heeded and every hunting party kept watch for enemies. For months Last Bull harbored resentments about this incident, and now, in the face of military emergency, he was determined to control not only the Elks but all the Cheyennes in the village. No one would be allowed to leave or even prepare breastworks.[50]

Elks and others gathered wood for the forced celebration fire and, when night fell, Kit Foxes compelled many to attend. Some mothers tied their daughters together to keep the men from trying to grab one and run off with her during the dance. A few of the men, defying the Kit Foxes, refused to participate in the celebration and occasionally climbed above the village looking for signs of an approaching enemy. Sits in the Night, at one point, slipped away to check on his horses and thought he detected someone lurking among them. He also thought he heard a rumbling noise down the stream—the ominous sounds of soldiers on the march.[51]

Just before daybreak, people drifted off toward their homes and beds. Heeding his father's warning, Brave Wolf removed neither his moccasins nor his clothes so that he would be ready to defend

49. Powell, *Sweet Medicine* 1:97. Little Wolf, Black Moccasins, and Old Bear were the 3 Old Man Chiefs who belonged to the Elk Scrapers Society. For more information on Cheyenne warrior societies, see Grinnell, *Fighting Cheyennes*, 218–19, and Hoebel, *Cheyennes*, 40–43.

50. Powell, *Sweet Medicine* 1:97; Powell, *People* 2:937–38.

51. Grinnell, *Fighting Cheyennes*, 375; Powell, *People* 2:1057.

the village if Box Elder's vision proved accurate. He felt that there was every reason to believe in it for Box Elder's prophecies always came true. Just as Brave Wolf began to doze, he heard the sharp report of distant gunfire.[52]

52. Stands in Timber, *Cheyenne Memories*, 216.

CHAPTER 4

The Battle

From the perspective of the charging soldiers and scouts, most of the Northern Cheyenne village lay to the south of the eastward flowing Red Fork. Smoke curled up from the tipis, which, arranged in an ellipse, stretched for nearly one mile along the thickly fringed banks of willow and cottonwood trees. In the frosty morning light the soldiers could discern steep, sturdy, red-sandstone hillsides on the northern and southern flanks of the village. On the west, the terrain sloped gently toward the surrounding mountains.

Just before the white men and their Indian allies heard the command to charge, Lieutenant John Bourke later recalled, "all the discontent and disquietude engendered during that night of cold and anxiety came to a head . . . our eyes nervously scanned the battlements behind which hostile sharp-shooters might within the next few hours be taking position. It might be our misfortune to have to fight our way back—who could tell?"[1]

Among those so preoccupied was Private Smith, who briefly mused on Custer's fate under similar circumstances earlier that year, but then realized. . . .

1. Bourke, *Mackenzie's Last*, 29.

[Dawn, November 25]

. . . but I did not feel a bit shakey. I dont [k]now why eather. I never took off my over coat for it was to cold. It was now day light and we started. We had room in the Pass to go in colloms of fours and the Indins at the head. We had not gone far when I looked up and saw an Indin on top of a big rock. He firred one shot and that was a signal that the Ball had opend. He was there as a sentinnal for the camp,[2] I suppose. He mounted his poney and lit out. It was now that our Indins set up the war hoop. This was the first time I had ever hird it in earnest. Then I was wild with excitement.

We started now on the charge but jest as we goot near the camp, the Indines [auxiliaries] turned up on the side of the mounten and this left us right to the front. Well this did not stop the Genroll and we dashed on. Now there was a bout 10 of us a way a hed of the collom. When the Indins [Northern Cheyennes] saw the Indins on the hill they all turned out and commenced a heavy fire on them. They had not seen us yet. When we were wright in to the camp, the Genral looked around and says We were all a lone. He goot a little excited and says go back and tell them companys to charge in hear. I went my self and went on the jump. I would of dashed in to the camp if he had of told me to jest now for the Bullets were flying every way and mity thick to. I had my Pistell in my hand and felt a little rattled, I must say, for this was the first time I had ever hird them so close.

As I was going around a hill I saw an old Indin and a boy makeing for the hill. I took a shot at him with my pistell and he caught hold of his leg and limped off. I don't know weather I hit him or not. As I come to each company, I told them what the Genrall sed and they dashed off at leighting [lightning] speed. It seemed as if the horses had goot new life. When I goot to the last Company I turned back and I never hird such a thunder of horses in all my life, for it was all rocks where we were.[3]

---

2. Cheyenne sources do not indicate the identity of this individual.

3. Lt. Bourke was equally impressed with the sounds of the charge, resorting to a curious mixture of natural and mechanical imagery in an attempt to recreate it: ". . . All was rush and clamor and shock, but the rush and clamor and shock of thoroughly organized pitiless war. . . . It was the rush of a mighty river, the roar of a giant engine, but each drop of water knew its destined channel, each element of the machine knew the function it had to perform." Bourke, Mackenzie's Last, 29.

At the head of the thundering column rode the Shoshones and Bannocks on one side, with the Pawnees on the other, and the Sioux, Cheyennes, and Arapahoes in the center. Within several hundred yards of the village, Colonel Ranald Mackenzie ordered Major Frank North and his Pawnee scouts to cross from the south bank of the Red Fork to the north in order to join the main body and to avoid the dangers of dividing the force. This, North later complained, slowed the charge, particularly when some Pawnee ponies became mired down in the creek bed, allowing the Northern Cheyennes more precious time to evacuate their families.[4] Meanwhile, Private Smith hurried back toward the village after relaying his message to the white soldiers to quicken their pace:

> . . . as I come in to the camp [the Northern Cheyenne village] and looking for the Gen., I looked up on a nole [knoll] wright over the camp and saw a man drest in a suit of Buckskin. I could not help but stop and watch him fireing in to the Indins. It turned out to bee a scout that they called Leittle buck Shot. One hundred of such men as him could whip more Indins than all the command poot togeather. Well I found the Genrall at last and saw M company scatter off. I then hird someone say Leut [John] McKiney was shot.[5] But not a word of lots of privits that I could se laying a round ded.

4. North, *Man of the Plains*, 213. See also Lessing H. Nohl, Jr., "Mackenzie Against Dull Knife: Breaking the Northern Cheyennes in 1876," in K. Ross Toole et al., eds., *Probing the American West: Papers from the Santa Fe Conference*, 88.

5. Since the Cheyennes wanted to keep as many of their horses out of enemy hands as possible, a small party of villagers had moved toward the plateau where several hundred of their ponies grazed. Understanding their purpose, Mackenzie ordered Lt. John McKinney to stop them. McKinney's advance was checked, however, by heavy fire that poured upon him and his men from a ravine sheltering a handful of Cheyenne sharpshooters. Six of their bullets slammed into the officer's body, while others felled his horse and 6 members of his command. Nohl, "Mackenzie Against Dull Knife," 89; Wheeler, *The Frontier Trail*, 174; and John Bourke diary, Nov. 25, 1876, Denver Public Library, 14–18.

Army doctor L. A. LaGarde recalled years later that soldiers brought Lt. McKinney to him still alive. When they laid him down in the makeshift hospital, he looked up at the doctor, uttered "Dr. LaGarde," mumbled something about his mother, and then died (Col. L. A. LaGarde, "At the Dinner of the Order of the Indian Wars, March 6, 1915," in Order of the Indian Wars Collection, L-2,

Lieutenant John McKinney, the only officer killed in the Dull Knife Battle, as a West Point cadet, class of 1871. Credit: United States Military Academy Archives

The Genral says go over and tell Capt. [Wirt] Davis[6] to make a charge with his company and take a hill. Jest as I goot there I hird some thing go pot and one of the men wright by me throde up his hands and droped off of his horse. I got out of hear and then watched this Company make the Charge. It was nice, for they all hung togeather like one man. They took a hill wright where Leut. McCinney was shot and cild [killed] a grate menney Indins hear.

U.S. Army Military History Institute, Carlisle Barracks, Pa.). Billy Garnett, the Sioux interpreter, recalled that McKinney died with a sword in his hand, adding, in what sounds like an apocryphal tale of the sort so common in frontier army annals: "From Fetterman to the time of his fall he had been boasting his intention, if he got in reach of an Indian on the campaign, to dispatch him with his sword. He started to redeem his promise," but was struck down ("Survey Notes, William Garnett at Cane Creek, S. D., 1907," Eli Seavey Ricker Collection, Nebraska State Historical Society, Box 4, Tablet 2, Roll 1, 11).
    Lt. John A. McKinney was born in Shelby County, Tenn., Oct. 4, 1847. He enrolled in the U.S. Army Military Academy at West Point in July 1867 and graduated 4 years later. In August 1871 he accepted a commission as second lieutenant in the 4th Cavalry and in May 1876 was promoted to first lieutenant. His brief military career ended Nov. 25, 1876. He was just barely 29 years old when he died. See John A. McKinney Military Service Record, File #6665 ACP 1876, Box 343, RG 94, Records of the Adjutant General's Office, NARS. See also Heitman, 1:673.
    6. As McKinney's men panicked and turned to flee, Mackenzie ordered Capt. John M. Hamilton and Capt. Davis to their rescue. In some of the day's hardest fighting, Davis's company, as Pvt. Smith noted, along with some of Hamilton's soldiers, charged the Cheyennes on foot, engaging in hand-to-hand combat and killing about 8 of their foe. Davis's men might have been wiped out had Lt. Walter Schuyler and his Shoshone scouts not taken a position on a craggy summit above the plateau and rained their bullets down on the Cheyennes. Nohl, "Mackenzie Against Dull Knife," 89; Bourke, *Mackenzie's Last*, 31–32; Bourke diary, Nov. 25, 1876, Denver Public Library, 1419.
    Wirt Davis's long military career spanned the years from the Civil War to the Spanish-American War at the close of that century. He first enlisted in the 4th Cavalry, May 12, 1860, at age 22. Although Virginia-born, Davis threw his lot in with the Union Army and for the next 40 years considered his official residence the army. Unlike many other officers on this expedition, Davis had not attended West Point. He rose through the ranks, starting as a private in 1860. Three years later he reached the position of commissioned officer when he was promoted to second lieutenant in the 4th Cavalry. In June 1868, Davis became a captain, the rank he carried into the Dull Knife Battle in 1876. He remained with the 4th Cavalry until 1890 when he was assigned as major, 5th Cavalry. More promotions followed rather quickly in the next decade, and when he re-

I went to the Gen. now and followed him a round. We were standing still once and the boolets were flying thick. When a fellow by the name of Foster,[7] one of the Ordleys, wrode up to me and says move around Smith or you will git shot. This is some thing I had never thought about before, for I was to much excited looking at some of the rest of the boys gitting shot and beeing carried down to the Hospitle. I forgot to say that when the Indins saw so meny soldiers comming over the hill they broke and run for the hills and this left us in a cross fire all day. When the Indins broke the squaws and young ons lit out for the timber and goot a way.

As the sun rose over the battlefield, various companies took position to prevent the Cheyennes from slipping in behind the troops and attacking the invaders from the rear. Others stormed through the village to force out sharpshooters still within, while another company occupied a small fringe of timber just beyond the village. Frank North and the Pawnees took possession of the mostly abandoned village itself. Although, as Smith noted, nearly all the women and children had been spirited out of the lodges and into the surrounding hills, the Cheyenne fighters did not retire from the field altogether. Instead, they held onto their natural fortifications in the high rocks, continued to level their careful aim at the soldiers and their allies, and waited for nightfall when they

---

tired in 1904, he did so as a recently appointed brigadier general. Davis's interests ranged beyond the military, however. He had studied French and Spanish at the University of Virginia before joining the army, and he also knew Italian. During his years on the frontier, he studied ornithology and zoology, although in a self-described "desultory way that did not interfere with military duties." As a result, he collected many specimens and had a fair knowledge of fauna in the United States. Davis received most accolades, though, for his military mettle. During his career he was breveted several times for gallant and meritorious service, including a brevet lieutenant-colonel rank for his part in the Dull Knife Battle (awarded in Feb. 1890). Davis died Feb. 11, 1904, in Washington, D.C., of chronic Bright's disease. Wirt Davis Military Service Record, File #4360 ACP 1878, Box 528, RG 94, NARS, and Heitman, *Historical Register*, 1:361.

7. This Foster was not listed on the Field Staff and Band Muster Roll, 4th Cavalry, for Nov. 1876. He was probably called up from one of the many companies of cavalry participating in this campaign, in the same manner as Smith. Private Smith may have made special note of his name since it was the same as his mother's maiden name.

might withdraw their families under cover of darkness.[8] In the meantime, Private Smith and the other orderlies were released from their duties:

> The boolets come so thick that the Genrol says you ordlys need not follow me around any more. So that left us to go where we wanted to. So I went down in among the teepes to see what I could find. For the Pawneys were plundering the camp. I went into one teepe and hear I found an old squaw with a nice pipe.[9] Well thinks I I must have that and so I make moshens to let me see it. But she would not do it. I could of shot hir but did not like to do that so when she stuck it out a little to one side I made a grab and caught it by the bowl and she hung onto the stem. She would of made at me now but I stuck my pistell in her fase and she did not like the looks of it and she lade down and roled up in a nice Buflow robe. I had a noshen to take that, but I went out and left hire to her fate.
>
> I poot the pipe in my pocket and went over to a company that had there horses in a river and left mine there and climed up on a hill where I could se all that was going on. I now thought I would take a few shots at some Indins I saw about 1 thousand yards off. I fired the shots I had in my belt and then, as I was laying there on my belley, I feel asleep.[10]

While Smith slept, Mackenzie, determined to save ammunition, gave stringent orders to stop all firing except at close range. During the long standoff only occasional exchanges of gunfire broke the eerie quiet. One soldier lifted his head and shoulders and immediately attracted the attention of a Cheyenne rifleman who, in Lieutenant Bourke's words, "put a bullet through his jaws; knocked him senseless against the bank in front of him. The blood

8. Bourke, *Mackenzie's Last*, 32; Bourke diary, Nov. 25, 1876, Denver Public Library, 1421; and Wheeler, *Frontier Trail*, 175.

9. Cheyenne sources do not reveal the identity of this woman.

10. Remarkable as his slumber in the midst of a battle may seem, one should remember that the troopers had participated in a forced march to this place and consequently spent a sleepless night preceding the fight. Luther North, with his brother Frank and the Pawnee scouts, had nearly missed the battle itself when, before the charge, he walked off to one side of the vast column as it waited for daylight, found a sheltered place behind a big rock, leaned against it, and fell asleep. Only when the Pawnees began to mount did he awake and join the fray. North, *Man of the Plains*, 212.

from his wound poured down his throat and choked him to
death."[11]

Even more dramatic was an event that Private Smith did
not apparently witness but that greatly impressed Lieutenant
Bourke (and perhaps ignited his imagination in retelling it for
publication):

> There was one notably daring warrior or chief, a powerful looking
> man, riding a fine white horse and himself bearing on his left arm
> a circular shield of buffalo hide and upon his head a war bonnet,
> whose pendant eagle plumes swept the ground at his horse's feet.
> Bullets struck the ground before him, behind him, beside him; the
> air groaned with the ominous whistle of Death's messengers; but
> each and all spared the grim Cheyenne who serenely rode along
> the front of our line, venting derision in the teeth of his foes, until
> the cool, deadly aim of Lieutenant Allison, of the 2d Cavalry,
> knocked him lifeless from his charger.
>
> Before the cheers from the whites and their Indian allies had
> died away, there issued from the Cheyenne line a young warrior
> gorgeous in his decorations of feathers, mounted upon a spirited
> pony, and bearing also upon his left arm a shield of buffalo hide,
> hardened in the fire and decorated with the plumage of the bald-
> headed eagle. This brave Cheyenne charged recklessly into the face
> of death, scorning the bullets which made the air hot around him,
> and chanting loudly the war-song proclaiming his determination
> to save from profane hands the corpse of his comrade and friend.
> On he flew, whipping into more energetic movement the faithful
> beast whose instinct warned it of imminent peril. Much sooner
> than it has taken to write this paragraph, he was bending over the
> bleeding form of the red-skinned Ajax, whose defiance was still
> sounding in our ears. Many were the expressions of admiration
> from our side as he lifted the body across the withers of the pony,
> and then springing lightly into the saddle, plied vigorously the
> quirt (or Indian whip of leather) and turned back to regain the
> friendly shelter of the rocks and gulches.
>
> Escape seemed secure, but Fate was only mocking the poor
> wretch. In War, business is business, and bullets must fall upon
> the just and unjust, the cowardly and the brave.
>
> Almost within a handshake of his people, the heroic Cheyenne

11. Bourke, *Mackenzie's Last*, 33.

and his sturdy pony, freighted with so precious a burden, bore testimony to the precision of our marksmen, and fell pierced with many wounds. They had been comrades in battle and in campaign; and in death they were not divided. "Greater love than this hath no man that he lay down his life for his friend." [12]

A small, grassy plateau separated soldiers from Cheyennes. When Private Smith awoke from his nap, he too raced his horse across this flat:

I don't [k]now how long I lay there but when I woke wright on my right side lay a fellow on his back ded with his mouth open. You bet I started to git away from hear. But found I could hardley move for my right leg was stiff. I limped off and found my hors and set there a while rubing my leg. I did not [k]now what to do for I did not want to go to the doctor with a little thing like this. So I goot on my hors and started a cross a flat and I believe there was one hundred shots fired at me. But I did not notice it for I was in sutch pane I did not care weather I goot shot or not.

I now went down behind our company and bathed my leg in the crick and this made me feel better. I then set there awhile and goot up and started to find hed quarters. I met the Genral and he asked me if I had been shot. I told him no and he sed no more. I went past the hospitle and a round the hill and hear I found the boys. They all had there dinner and the Pack tranc had goot in. So I goot myself something to eate the first bite in 24 ours [hours]. As soon as I eate I fed my little horse for he was near gone up. Some of the boys were mity sick [wounded] and I did not say mutch about my leg.

The Indins had stuck up a white flag two or three times in the day but the Genral did not see it and the boys would shoot at it.

---

12. Ibid., 33–34. See also Wheeler, *Frontier Trail*, 174. Cheyenne sources do not include testimony about this event, and Luther North suggests that Bourke embellished a bit in retelling it, noting, for example, that the Cheyenne men involved in this incident did not wear headdresses. Nevertheless, such actions in battle were not uncommon. For more information on Cheyenne methods and manners of warfare, see Hoebel, *Cheyennes*, 77–80, and Grinnell, *Fighting Cheyennes*, 12. Bourke's account is useful in demonstrating the rather romanticized view some army officers had of Indian warfare and bravery in battle. See Sherry L. Smith, "'Civilization's Guardians': U.S. Army Officers' Reflections on Indians and the Indian Wars in the Trans-Mississippi West, 1848–1890" (Ph.D. diss., University of Washington, 1984), 143–45.

About this time Frank Gurrard [Grouard][13] our scout came up and sed that the Indins sed if the soldiers would stop firring that they would. So the Genrol gave orders to cease firring. Now every thing was quiet and pooty soon there was a white flag stuck up and the Gen. told Gurrard to go and se what they wanted. They told him if the Gen. would give them their Poyenes [ponies] that they would Surrender. But the Gen. told them he could not give them there ponies. So they told him to come and take them that he had cild [killed] most all of them and he could cill the rest. I gess there had been about 100 cilld and I don't [k]now how many wounded.[14]

By this time everyone knew clearly that the Northern Cheyennes did not intend to surrender. After consulting with officers and Indian allies, Mackenzie decided to move all captured ponies and destroy the village. Although tempted to charge up the mountain in order to drive the Northern Cheyennes out of the

13. Frank Grouard had lived with the Hunkpapa Sioux Sitting Bull for 5 years before he began working as a scout for the army. He scouted for Crook earlier in 1876 and participated in the Battle of the Rosebud. See Utley, *Frontier Regulars,* 236, 256, 270.

14. Smith's estimate of the Cheyenne dead was much too high, and his testimony concerning the truce talks differed from Bourke's. According to this officer, during a lull in the action scout Bill Rowland, some half-bloods, and some Cheyenne scouts moved closer to the Northern Cheyennes to talk. Initially the latter seemed more interested in greeting these men with bullets than in parlaying, but eventually they did discuss surrender. Morning Star, they reported, was prepared to stop fighting, since he had already lost several sons in the battle, but Little Wolf, Roman Nose, Gray Head, and Old Bear were determined to continue their defense. These men also told the scouts, "'Go home, you have no business here. We can whip the white soldiers alone, but can't fight you too.'" Other Cheyennes approached and threatened to seek assistance from a nearby Sioux village where their friends would help them wipe out the troops and their Indian allies. They, too, however seemed resigned. "You have killed and hurt a heap of our people," they said, "you may as well stay now and kill the rest of us." According to Peter Powell, Morning Star lost two sons in this battle, one shot by Captain Luther North at the outset of the battle and another whose body was found lying across the stream southwest of his father's camp. Bourke maintained that one of these sons was actually a son-in-law. Peter J. Powell, *Sweet Medicine* 1:164; Bourke, *Mackenzie's Last,* 35. For information on William Worland, an Anglo-American scout married to a Southern Cheyenne woman, see a short biographical statement in "A Day with the 'Fighting Cheyennes,'" *Motor Travel Magazine* (June 1930): 17.

rocks, Mackenzie weighed the possible gains of such a move against the loss of human lives. Deciding against such a strategy, he sent for help from Crook and the infantry, whose more powerful rifles could be brought to bear upon the Cheyennes in the strongholds, should they still be there the next morning and the days after that.[15]

Meanwhile, Private Smith decided to take one more stroll through the village:

Well there was no more firring done to amount to anything and I took a walk down among the teepes. Our Indins had birnt a good menney of them. I come to the teepe where I had goot the pipe in the morning. And hear I saw the old squaw shot all to pieces. I found after words that some of the boys in my company had done it for to get the Bufflow robe. I saw lots of ded Indins now laying a round all over. I went back and watched the boys carring in the ded and wounded some skelpt and some striped of all their clothing. Among them was 3 out of our company one by the name of Kellie [Edward Kelly][16] was kild and two by the nams of Strick [Augustus Strick][17] and Buck [Edwin S. Buck][18] were wounded.

15. Bourke, *Mackenzie's Last*, 35; North, *Man of the Plains*, 216.
16. Edward Kelly had enlisted in the army only several months before this battle, signing up Aug. 11, 1876, at Baltimore, Md. Standing 5 feet, 7 inches tall, with blue eyes, sandy brown hair, and a ruddy complexion, this former teamster was 30 years old when he joined the military service. Contrary to Smith's account, Kelly did not die. He remained in the army for his full 5-year enlistment and was honorably discharged at Fort Supply, Indian Territory, Aug. 1881. "Register of Enlistments in the U.S. Army, 1798–1914," M–223, 74:256, NARS. The only man from Smith's company who died in the battle was Alexander Keller. The similarity of names explains Smith's error.
17. Before enlisting in the army at Chicago in 1875, Strick worked as a clerk. He had gray eyes, light-colored hair, a fair complexion, and stood 5 feet, 6 and one-half inches tall. Strick had been born in New York City, 24 years before the Dull Knife Battle. He survived the battle but was discharged from the army on March 26, 1877, at Camp Robinson for disabilities due to his injuries from the fight. "Register of Enlistments," M–233, 76:275, NARS.
18. Edwin S. Buck was born in Williamsport, Pa., and was a 29-year-old laborer when he enlisted in the army at St. Louis, Mo., in Aug. 1876. He stood 5 feet, 3 inches tall, and had hazel eyes, dark brown hair, and a ruddy complexion. He too was discharged from the army at Camp Robinson in March 1877 for disabilities resulting from the Dull Knife Battle. "Register of Enlistments," M–233, 72:184, NARS.

Altogether, one officer and six enlisted men died in the engagement, while twenty-five soldiers and Indian scouts were wounded.[19] The number of Northern Cheyennes killed and wounded was more difficult for army officials to determine, but Colonel Mackenzie reported twenty-five enemy dead, while Lieutenant W. P. Clark estimated two Cheyenne women and fourteen men were killed.[20] The most crushing blow to the Cheyennes, however, came with the destruction of their village at the hands of the army and its Indian allies. Colonel Mackenzie had learned

19. George Crook to Adjutant General, U.S. Army, December 1, 1876, Box 1810, RG 94, Records of the Adjutant General's Office, 1780s–1917, Letters Received, NARS. Those killed in the battle included Lt. John A. McKinney, Cpl. Patrick F. Ryan, Pvt. James Baird, Pvt. John Sullivan, Pvt. Alexander Keller, Pvt. John Menges, and Pvt. Alexander McFarland. McFarland died on November 28 of wounds received in the battle.

20. See George Crook to Philip Sheridan, Nov. 28, 1876, Box 1810, RG 94, Records of the Adjutant General's Office, 1780s–1917, Letters Received, NARS. In this telegram Crook sent Mackenzie's first report of the battle and estimate of the enemy dead. Lieutenant Clark's estimate of Cheyenne casualties was based on statements made to him by Cheyennes who surrendered at Red Cloud and Spotted Tail agencies in the months following the fight. The reason casualties were relatively light, Clark explained, was that an Indian man "has a wonderful faculty of protecting himself and unless he is shot through the brain, heart or back, there is no certainty at all about his dying, for since I have seen many Indians here who have been shot in all manner of ways through the body and still enjoying excellent health, I have been convinced that of all animals they are the superior in point of tenacity of life, magnificent horsemen and fine shots—doing about as good execution on the backs of their thoroughly-trained, speedy and hardy ponies as on the ground, accustomed from their earliest youth to take advantage of every knoll, rock, tree, tuft of grass and every aid the topography of the country affords to secure game, and their education completed and perfected by constant warfare with other tribes and the whites" See Lt. W. P. Clark, "Report of the Sioux War," Sept. 14, 1877, Doc. #4601, RG 393, Department of the Platte, Letters Received, NARS. The largest number of Cheyennes died in the gulch near where Lieutenant McKinney died. Among the Cheyenne men killed at this spot were Stump, Red Winged Woodpecker, Split Eye, Bull Hump, Red Burn, Walking Calf, Hawk or Hawk's Visit, Four Ma?heono, Old Bull, and Antelope. See Powell, People 2:1061. Bourke claimed 30 Cheyennes were left on the battlefield and that, upon surrender, the Cheyennes submitted a list of 40 killed. See Bourke, Mackenzie's Last, 35. A number of historians have accepted his testimony, including Utley, Frontier Regulars, 275; Nohl, "Mackenzie Against Dull Knife," 90; and Powell, Sweet Medicine 1:164.

on the southern plains the importance of thoroughly destroying villages as a wartime measure. Now he brought that lesson to wintry Wyoming, where it would have an even deadlier effect. This village consisted of about two hundred lodges, most of them canvas, some of them buffalo hide. Bourke maintained that each was a virtual "magazine of ammunition, fixed and loose, and a depot of supplies of every mentionable kind." He was a military man with an ethnologist's sensitivities, and so he understood that every lodge was also a Cheyenne home and a place of beauty. As the soldiers and scouts began their ruinous purpose on the afternoon of November 25, Bourke lamented that men "detailed upon a work of destruction have no time for indulgence in the contemplation of the aesthetic development of savages . . . wiping off the face of the earth many products of aboriginal taste and industry which would have been gems in the cabinets of museums." They hastily dismantled the tipis, split the lodgepoles into smaller fragments, and flung them onto what, Bourke wrote, "it is no rhetorical flourish to call the funeral pyres of Cheyenne glory."[21]

To the Northern Cheyennes who watched their homes burn from the vantage point of their rimrock refuge, the scene must have deepened their growing sense of despair. In the frightful excitement of the soldiers' stampede at dawn, most women and children secured safe positions in the mountains above the village, but as they fled their homes they had failed to grab robes and blankets for protection from the cold. Brave Wolf and others eventually built fires to provide warmth for those nearly half-frozen. As they huddled near the flames, then, they watched the soldiers and Indian allies below burn their tipis, their winter provisions, their robes, their clothing—everything they owned.[22]

At this point, the Northern Cheyennes turned to the power of the Sacred Arrows. Men and women gathered around Black Hairy Dog, Sacred Arrow keeper, who had found a vantage point above the village. There he spread white sage on the ground, took the Sacred Arrows from their kit-fox–skin wrapping, and laid them in a row upon the sage so that the arrows faced the distant enemy

21. Bourke, *Mackenzie's Last*, 36, 39.
22. Stands in Timber, *Cheyenne Memories*, 217.

Dull Knife (seated) and Little Wolf were both in the village on the Red Fork of the Powder River when cavalry troops attacked. Credit: National Anthropological Archives, Smithsonian Institution

soldiers and scouts. Black Hairy Dog stamped the ground four
times and made noises reminiscent of a buffalo, while the others
shouted in defiance and stamped the ground as well. These
sounds encouraged the other Cheyennes, who fought with renewed courage, for they now knew the power of the Sacred Arrows was turned against their foe.[23]

At one point during the battle, a lone Indian rode out from the
ranks of the invaders, carrying a large amount of ammunition. He
reached a knoll not far from where Black Hairy Dog was pointing
the Sacred Arrows toward the enemy. The Cheyennes recognized
him as Old Crow, one of their own, one of the esteemed Council
of Forty-four, who was now scouting for the soldiers. Old Crow
shouted, "I must fight with [i.e., against] you; but I am leaving a
lot of ammunition on the hill." Later the Cheyennes found a huge
pile of cartridges there, but for years after they scorned this chief,
who they believed had betrayed his own kinsmen.[24]

Of these human dramas, Private Earl Smith remained oblivi-
ous. To him, the Northern Cheyennes were anonymous targets.
He did not know their names, their faces, their families, their
pasts. Nor did they know his. It was only when confronted with
an individual Cheyenne, the old woman in her lodge, that he at
least momentarily grasped their humanity. And in that brief col-
lision with reality in the form of a decrepit woman unable to flee
for her life, he encountered his own humanity, for he could not
bring himself to kill her, even though she was, ostensibly, an
"enemy." One can only speculate what he thought of the "boys"
who did kill her "for to get the Bufflow robe."

What he did record was a poem that allowed him to transcend
thoughts of bloodshed, tragedy, and even murder in order to present the battle as an heroic event. To see the day's activities as
honorable, moral, and even noble certainly met the psychic needs
of Private Smith and some others who fought with him. Smith

23. Ibid., 217. Stands in Timber said that all Mackenzie's Cheyenne scouts
were dead by 1885 because the Sacred Arrows were turned against them this
day. See also Powell, *Sweet Medicine* 1:158–59.

24. Powell, *People* 2:1065; Stands in Timber, *Cheyenne Memories*, 217; and
Karen Easton, "Getting into Uniform: Northern Cheyenne Scouts in the United
States Army, 1876–81" (Master's thesis, University of Wyoming, 1985), 51.

and the other soldiers had functioned as professionals who found personal and group actions worthy of glorification. They avenged the death of other Anglo-American soldiers. They did their job, were victorious, and perhaps most significantly, they survived unharmed.

The Red Rock Canon Fight

Twas in camp we lay as you quickly shall hear
Mckenzie came to us and bade us prepare
Saying saddle your horses by the setting sun
For the Indians were laying in Red Rock Canon.

We saddled our horses and away we did go
Over rivers of ice and mountains of snow
To the Red Rock Canon our course we did stear
It was the Fourth Horse who had never known fear.

We rode all that night 'til the daylight did break
When the herd from the Cheyennes the Pawnees did take
But the squaws they escaped, papooses and all
For we wasn't in time to capture them all.

The Indians formed up, the fight it began
They thought they could frighten the bold white man
With our glistning arms right at them we sped
They turned tail about, to the rocks they all fled.

We soon overtook them as frightened they fled
Cut off the long hair they wore on their head
"No mercy" "No Mercy" so loud was our cry
Have vengeance for Custer brave soldiers or die.

Mid snow on the rocks the Indians lay dead
Over thirty were scalped and the rest of them fled.
Six hundred dragoons made thousands to yield
Their chiefs soon likewise lay dead on the field.

McKenzie came to us and this he did say
"I thank you brave boys for your valor today."
Catch up your horses and feed everyone
For the fight it is over and the battle is done.

"Here's success to McKenzie" so endeth our stave
Likewise Captain Hamphill an officer brave

With a full flowing glass we'll drink and let wring
Success to the Fourth horse so loud let us sing.

The 25 of November my boys was the day
When six hundred dragoons made those Indians run away
Although they did number eight hundred or more
We'll drink and we'll sing now the battle is O'er.[25]

The army troops fought, the poem argues, not to force
Cheyenne surrender of the Powder River country so that Anglo-
Americans might claim it, but to avenge George Armstrong Custer and his brave soldiers. Lest one think this interpretation was
the stuff of only enlisted men's folklore, Lieutenant Bourke's account included a detailed listing of all artifacts found within the
Northern Cheyenne village that implicated some of these people
in the June 25 fight on the Little Bighorn, as well as the scalps of
two young girls (one Caucasian, the other Shoshone), a buckskin
bag containing the right hands of twelve Shoshone babies, and a
necklace of human fingers.[26] To the American soldiers, and to the
Shoshone auxiliaries, these articles alone justified the punishment
meted out to the Northern Cheyennes that day.

To be sure, the Northern Cheyennes did not see matters the
same way. The saddles and canteens branded with Seventh Cavalry insignia, the scalps, the necklace of fingers—all represented
Cheyenne victories over constant enemies who had, on other oc-
casions, done the same to them. Some of their enemies scalped
Northern Cheyennes on this day as they lay upon the battlefield.
And what, some may have thought, could be more cruel than
destroying Cheyenne homes in the winter and putting to the torch
all their beautiful things? "Never again," wrote one historian,
"would Northern Cheyenne material culture reach the heights of
richness and splendor that the people knew before that bitter day
in the Big Horn's."[27]

25. In the original diary a notation at the end of the poem reads: "Copied
Sept. 16, 1877, by Chas. S. Fowler for Wm. E. Smith, Co. E, 4th Cav., Ft.
Wallace, Kansas."
26. Bourke, *Mackenzie's Last*, 39–41; Bourke diary, Nov. 26, 1876, Denver
Public Library, 1429–32.
27. Powell, *Sweet Medicine* 1:167.

As night fell, the Pawnees assumed their post in the ransacked village where sharpshooters from the mountainside allowed them little sleep. The Shoshone scouts did not rest either as they wept and sang. They were grieving because they reasoned (from things found in the village) that the Cheyennes had just returned from destroying one of their villages in the Wind River range.[28] Finally, Private Smith and Colonel Mackenzie, too, spent a troubled, restless night in the valley of the Red Fork:

Nov. 25th 1876

It was near nite now and the Gen. says boys make down your bedds a long hear in a row for the Indins will atact [attack] us a gane to nite This camp was in a kind of a bason and a fine stream runing threw it wright in the senter of the Big horn Mtn. On both sids the mountanes rose up 1 thousand feet high and off red rock and at one end was a long hill covered with fine trees. This is where all the squoows goot out and we could not take the woods.

They put a strong gard on to nite and I went to bed more ded than alive. We were rite near the hospitle and I could hear the wounded groneing all nite. I could not sleep mitch for my leg now was gitting worse and every time I woke I could see the Genrall walking up and down. I don't believe he slept a bit that nite. His mind must of been trubled about some thing. I don't [k]now what, for he is the bravest man I ever saw. He dont seem to think any more about boolets flying than I would about snowballs. We had in all cilled 11 and wounded 28.[29] This mad quite a lot. Well, this ended the 25 of Nov. and I was glad to see Nite.

28. Bourke, *Mackenzie's Last*, 42.
29. Smith was mistaken on the number of army killed, which totaled 7, not 11.

CHAPTER 5

Return to Crazy Woman

For Lieutenant Colonel Richard Dodge, back at Crazy Woman's Fork, November 25 began and ended quite differently than it had for Private Smith. The Colonel rose rather late that day, composed a long letter to a loved one, and feeling the need for exercise, went hunting with several other officers. Nearly two and one-half miles away from camp, the party encountered General Crook, alone except for his horse, peeking in the sagebrush for rabbits. The scene reinforced Dodge's conviction that Crook was not only foolhardy and thoughtless, but unsuited for command. "He will be picked off some day," Dodge grumbled in his diary. "He is as reckless as Custer in a different way. Custer was all dash and daring when there was anything to be made by it, in glory, or public opinion. Crook is just as daring, but in pursuits of his own quiet enjoyment in hunting."[1] Once back in camp, the rather eventless day ended for Dodge with several games of whist, and then sound sleep. There was no news of Mackenzie.

Next morning, General Crook roused Dodge from his trestle bed with word of Mackenzie's fight and of the Northern Cheyennes' potentially troublesome position in the rocks, where as Bourke put it, "One Indian is equal to 10 Cavalrymen."[2] Anxious

1. Dodge diary, Nov. 25, 1876, Newberry Library.
2. Quoted in Dodge diary, Nov. 26, 1876, Newberry Library.

89

to finish the matter, Crook ordered Dodge and his men out as
soon as possible with two days' rations and one hundred rounds
of ammunition. The general intended to join the fray as well.
They got off by noon and, hampered by a fresh snow fall three
inches deep, followed the horsemen's route of several days before.
After eleven hours of hard marching, the infantrymen bivouacked
in the snow. Dodge's description of the countryside echoed the
words of Smith, although Dodge's language was certainly more
sophisticated:

> The trail was so narrow that the Command had to move in single
> file, sometimes it ran diagonally around a steep slope, when if a
> man slipped he was out of ranks at once and had to get in where
> he could. In going down one almost precipice one fellow slipped,
> fell on his bottom and gliding swiftly forward was set upon by at
> least thirty men. A whole Company was down in an indiscriminate
> heap and the snowing was something terrific. We were blessed
> with about a ten days old moon, but its light was fitful in the
> extreme. Clouds were constantly passing over it, and always (it
> seemed) just when we were in the worst places. The scene was
> weird and picturesque in the extreme. Far as the eye could reach
> to the south and east and north [one could see] only the unbroken
> snow, wreathed in all uncouth and fantastic shapes by the broken
> crags and yawning ravines it covered. To the west [were] the huge
> piles of the Big Horn Mountains, here bare and white, there black
> with its forests of pine. Bad as it all was, everybody (almost) was
> in good spirits. I felt first rate, and except that I had to walk down
> all the steep ravines (my horse being smooth shod) and lead my
> horse at the risk of having him slide on top of me, I got along first
> rate. I don't like walking at any time, and I took some promenades
> on that night that I shall remember all my life.[3]

The doughboys dropped down into the valley of Willow Creek,
a tributary of the Powder, where they overtook General Crook.
There the infantry camped in drifts of snow about one foot deep,
according to Dodge's estimation. And it was there that Dodge
offered the following, providing an officer's view of his orderly:

> We got a little dry willow and made a rousing fire considering
> the quantity and quality of the wood. In a little while my Or-
> derly—Cook—a private of I Company, had a good cup of coffee

3. Ibid.

which with cold fried bacon and frozen bread constituted our supper, and a most toothsome and enjoyable one it was. Cook is a character. He was my orderly in the Black Hills, being then a private in a Cavalry Company. He was transferred to the Infantry, being ruptured and unable to do hard service on horseback. He has not the slightest idea of politeness—no bump of reverence—never thinks of saying "Sir" to anybody and speaks of officers as Crook and Mackenzie without a thought of giving them their official title. But he is perfectly invaluable—a splendid hostler, a fair cook, an eye like a hawk for game—is thoroughly honest—that is he would only steal for me, if I needed anything. He never forgets or loses anything—is always rough and always ready for anything.[4]

Earlier that day another colonel and his orderly-cook shared a cup of coffee. Colonel Ranald Mackenzie and Private William Earl Smith began that morning huddled over their campfire in the Big Horn Mountains. Difference in rank and concerns about military etiquette temporarily were put aside by the drama of the recent combat, and the two men, comrades in arms, drank their coffee and talked while the rest of the camp slept:

Sunday Nov. 26th 1876

I awoke in the morning after my ressless Nits sleep and goot breackfast reddy for I had to bee up before anybody else. While I was cooking the Genrall come to me and asked me if I was sick durring the nite. He sed I did not sleep much. I node by this that he had not slept a toll durring the nite. I asked him if he would have a coop of coffe and he sed he would. While he was drinking he talked to me a good deal about the fite a [and] seemed to feel bad about the boys that had been hirt and ciled.

Now the bugal sounded for the first time in this camp and every body was astir. Breakfast all over the Gen. gave orders to birn every thing in the camp and pack up. I forgoot to say we had lost one of our packmuls and a lot of the Gen's things were on it and all so my blankets and that left me with only two I had on my horse. Ever thing was a mooving around the hospitle making travose [travois] to carrey the wounded on and straping the ded on mules for the boddies were frose stiff.

Troopers and Indian allies awoke to a wintry scene. Luther North, for one, thought he was smothering under his buffalo robe

4. Ibid.

and upon pushing it off, felt "about a half a bushel of snow" tumble down his neck.[5] As snow flurries fell, soldiers and scouts finished destroying the village and every piece of property they could find in it, including untanned buffalo robes, skins, and blankets. Pots, tin cups, plates, coffee pots, kettles, and other culinary implements became targets for soldiers' axes.[6] The Northern Cheyennes would have to make their way to friendly sanctuary without benefit of these items. A good number of years later Luther North would remember the devastation as well as the bitterly cold temperatures. "Those poor Cheyennes," he wrote, "were out in that weather with nothing to eat, no shelter (we had burned their village) and hardly any clothing. It was said many children died. It makes me sort of sick to think of it."[7]

How did the Cheyennes cope? During the night Two Moon approached several lodges pitched away from the main camp, that had not been burned. There he found three buffalo robes—a welcome addition to the pitifully few garments his people had to protect themselves from the elements.[8] They were not enough. A number of Cheyenne children froze to death that first night in the mountains. Three more perished the next night. The now homeless Cheyennes slaughtered several horses for food. They killed others so that old men and women could place their freezing hands and feet in the animals' steaming entrails. Only a few had escaped from the village with moccasins, so they wrapped their

5. North, *Man of the Plains*, 217.
6. Bourke diary, Nov. 26, 1876, Denver Public Library, 1429.
7. North, *Man of the Plains*, 217; Lt. W. P. Clark reported the following spring that, "Infants died of cold at their mothers' breasts, fourteen men, women and children were badly frozen." See "Report of the Sioux War," RG 393, Department of the Platte, Letters Received, NARS, Sept. 14, 1877, Doc. #4601. Lt. Bourke wrote that 11 Cheyenne babies froze to death "in the arms of famished mothers, and ponies had to be killed that feeble old men and women might prolong their lives by inserting feet and legs in the warm entrails." See Bourke, *Mackenzie's Last*, 35. The army officers' numbers were only estimates. Cheyenne sources do not indicate the number of Cheyennes who survived the battle but then died from exposure in the days following the fight. Peter Powell offers the figure of 11 babies killed but relies on John Bourke for this number. See Powell, *Sweet Medicine* 1:167.
8. Grinnell, *Fighting Cheyennes*, 381.

feet in whatever they could find—cloth, skins, buffalo hides, and animal carcasses. Among the fugitives was White Frog, who ached from three bullet wounds, and his wife, Comes Together, who kept her infant son close to her body to warm him with her own heat—a son who would survive and one day become Keeper of the Sacred Buffalo Hat.[9] Before daybreak, all began to move in the direction of Crazy Horse's village, somewhere to the northeast, where they hoped to find refuge and relief.[10]

Most of the white men on the battlefield that morning thought more about their own suffering, and that of the wounded among their own ranks, than they did the Cheyennes. The greatest care, under the circumstances, was given to those soldiers and scouts with injuries. During the night, the healthy stoked large fires to keep the wounded comfortable and to provide light for the construction of travois. With lodgepoles and buffalo robes secured from the Northern Cheyennes' village, they hastily built thirty travois or litters to carry the sick and wounded back to Crazy Woman Creek. Each man was lifted onto a travois and painstakingly carried out of the valley. The travois offered little jolting and the advantage of keeping the wounded man's head above the rest of his body. In this way, he remained relatively comfortable.[11]

Nothing could be done for the dead. One man was buried on the battlefield.[12] The rest, their bodies frozen hard, were slung over the backs of pack mules, which, at first, seemed "restive and frightened," according to Lieutenant John Bourke, but eventually became "reconciled to their ghastly cargoes."[13] At last all was ready, as Smith reported:

> We finly broke camp a bout 11 Oclock and started out of this dedly valley and I was glad to git a way. We marched 7 mils and camped on Rock crick, the same one the fite was on. Hear our Indins had

9. Powell, *Sweet Medicine* 1:167–68.

10. Lt. Bourke claimed Indian scouts working for the army found the Cheyennes about 6 miles from the battlefield the morning after the fight. Bourke diary, Nov. 26, 1876, Denver Public Library, 1432.

11. Homer W. Wheeler, *The Frontier Trail: Or From Cowboy to Colonel*, 178–81.

12. This was Pvt. James Baird, D Company, 4th Cavalry.

13. Bourke, *Mackenzie's Last*, 42.

a skelp dance and I went over to see it. They had a good meny
and they made the valey ring with there shouts. The camp Was
Well garded to nite for fear of a surprise and the Wounded Were
resting well.

Next day, the soldiers remained skittish, uncertain of the enemy's position. Smith went on:

Monday Nov. 27th

Broke camp earley and made 15 mils and camped on a fork of the
Powder river. This was a hard day for the wounded for they had
to go over a ruff cuntry and hear we hird that Gen. Crook was
near us with all the Infatry. He had hird that we were in a place
and could not git out. He had marched the Infrontry 35 mils over
the cuntry and nearly cripled them all.
This nite jest after supper there was a stampeed [fear of an Indian
attack] among the soldiers. I had a nice big fire, for I was baking
breed [bread] and one of the boys wanted to poot it out. I told him
to git away dam quick to for I was mity sick of Indins by this time
for beeing up nite and day cooking and near frose to death. I went
to my hors that was laireted [tied up] near the fire and my carbine
was there saddle and all. I poot my belt on and sidelinde my Poney
and then set down on my saddle witch was on the Picket Pin and
waited to see what was comming. I had 1 hundred rounds of shots
in my saddle Pockets and I dont belive I could of been mad to
leave hear if I had of been shot right hear. But I would of been a
bad peace of meat jest now to of took. It had been snowing all day
and was very cold. The stampeed was caused by some Indins [al-
lies] shooting Buflow. And some of this [buffalo meat] we goot the
next day. Baked my Bred.

Sergeant James S. McClellan's journal revealed similar concerns
that day over Indian attacks on the retreating column:

We expected an attack today as the scouts reported another large
village to the west and as we were the last company of the rear
guard, I felt uneazy for fear they would cut us of[f]. Lots of horses
gave out and were shot along the trail. Our horses are very week,
and, the snow that has been falling the past two mornings makes
the road very slippery. We marched 14 miles and camped on a
fork of the Powder River. When in camp about two hours a herd
of buffalo came in to the Indian Scouts camp and they fired a

volley into them. We of course thought it was another attack but soon found out what it was.[14]

As Mackenzie and his men marched east toward CrazyWoman Creek, Crook and the infantrymen moved west. On November 27, five Indian couriers from Mackenzie met the general with news that the cavalrymen had decamped the day before and were bringing the killed and wounded out of the mountains. Crook then ordered Dodge to countermarch his column.[15] Not until the next day, however, did General Crook receive Colonel Mackenzie's report of operations against the Cheyennes, which he quickly forwarded to General Philip Sheridan, along with his own view of the situation. He could not resist a bit of hyperbole thinking, no doubt, not only of Mackenzie's reputation but his own as well. "I can't commend too highly," Crook crowed, "his [Mackenzie's] brilliant achievements and the gallantry of the troops of his command. This will be a terrible blow to the hostiles as these Cheyennes were not only the bravest warriors but have been head and front of most all the raids and deviltry committed in this country."[16]

Mackenzie's presentation of the matter, the first word the outside world would read of the battle, was straightforward, limited to the facts, and garnished only with the obligatory commendation of the officer who died:

> Sir: I have the honor to report that at about twelve o'clock AM, on the twenty fourth (24th) inst. while marching in a south westerly direction towards the Sioux Pass of the Big Horn Mountains I was met by five (5) of the seven (7) indian scouts who had been sent out the evening before who reported that they had discovered the

14. James S. McClellan Journal, Nov. 27, 1876, typescript copy loaned to author by Thomas R. Buecker, Fort Robinson Historic Site, Nebr. Original journal located at New York Public Library.

15. Dodge diary, Nov. 27, 1876, Newberry Library.

16. George Crook to Philip Sheridan, Nov. 28, 1876, Box 1810, RG 94, Records of the Adjutant General's Office, 1780s–1917, Letters Received, NARS. In his diary Lt. Col. Dodge noted that Crook visited him and they had a long talk about the battle: "He thinks the fighting over and that Crazy Horse will now either surrender, or decamp and hide himself in the bad lands. He is much pleased with his success." See Dodge diary, Nov. 28, 1876, Newberry Library.

main camp of the Cheyennes at a point in the mountains, about fifteen or twenty miles distant. Two of the seven (7) indians remaining to watch their camp, the command was halted near sunset and then moved toward the village intending to reach it at or before daylight, owing to the nature of the country, which was very rough and in some places difficult to pass with Cavalry. The command did not reach the village until about half an hour after daylight. The surprise was, however, almost complete. The approach to the village, the only practicable one, entered the lower end and the indians taking alarm took refuge in a network of very difficult ravines, beyond the upper end of the village, leaving it on foot and taking nothing but their arms with them. A brisk fight for about an hour ensued after which shooting was kept up until night. The village consisting of one hundred and seventy three (173) lodges and their entire contents were destroyed. About five hundred (500) ponies were taken & twenty-five (25) indians killed whose bodies fell into our hands. And from reports which I have no reason to doubt, I believe a much larger number were killed. Our loss was one (1) officer and five (5) men killed & twenty five (25) soldiers & one (1) Shoshone indian wounded. Fifteen (15) cavalry horses and four horses belonging to indian scouts were killed. The command remained in the village during the night and moved to this point today. Lieut. McKinney, Fourth (4th) Cavalry who was killed in this affair was one of the most gallant officers and honorable men that I have ever known.[17]

Had Private Smith read this special commendation, he might have noted, as he did during the battle itself, "not a word of lots of privits" that died—a group which by November 28 included Private Alexander McFarland, who succumbed that day to wounds received in the fight.[18] Lieutenant Homer Wheeler, in charge of the dead and wounded, later recalled that when McFarland stopped breathing, his body was strapped onto a mule and his travois given over to Anzi, a Shoshone scout suffering from a severe intestinal wound. Although doctors did not expect Anzi to live, he had mounted his horse and joined the other scouts when they first left the battlefield. Now he found he could no longer ride and gratefully accepted the travois. One of

17. Crook to Sheridan, Nov. 28, 1876, Box 1810, RG 94, NARS. I have added some punctuation to aid the reader.
18. Pvt. Alexander McFarland had belonged to Company L, 5th Cavalry.

McFarland's friends, who belonged to his company and had been taking care of him, pleaded with Wheeler not to put his dead bunkie on the mule. But the officer replied that Anzi was an ally and that he was obliged to take care of him as well as he could—that, in fact, had Anzi been an enemy he would have felt equally compelled to attend his needs.[19]

On this day, Smith seemed most concerned with his own trials—deepening snows and plunging temperatures.

Tuesday Nov. 28th 1876

Left this campt day light and made 16 mils and went in to camp on a branch of crasy Womns fork. The nite the snow was about 2 feet deep on a level and I fell into the crick and goot all wet while gitting water for supper. I goot pooty dry before I went to bed. It was so cold I could hardly sleep.

Wensday Nov. 29th 1876

Broke camp and marched 10 mils and come to our suply trane and was mity glad to git in our tents agane. I had far drother sleep in a tent than outdoors in the snow. And hear it was that I saw my old friend Sargent Magor Welch and I told him I wanted to git out of the cooking for I had been in over my turn now for 10 days was as long as We Were to cook. Well he says I will se and he says git supper any Way. I goot super and Sed nomore and goot Breakfast. You see I turned out to bee such a good cook that he would not realeve me. After Breackfast I told him I Would not cook another meal and he says God dam your soul I will make you cook. I says look hear dont you cus me anymore now I have had a nuff of it. I would of shot him then in a minute. He sed no more and told a nother man to go in the cook house and I would show him how to Bake Bred. And this old Courd of a Son of a B went to the Gen. and had a talk and I node [knowed] it was about me. Well this nite I poot in in my tent by a fire.

Thursday the 30th 1876

Thanksgiving Day. I had a little longer to sleep now and I poot it in. Well had nothing to do but git up and take care of my horse and go and eate my Breacfast. We had an reglor old thanksgiving

19. Wheeler, *Frontier Trail*, 182–83. Anzi remained in the post hospital at Cantonment Reno for 2 or 3 weeks and then rode his horse home to Fort Washakie Agency, at least 200 miles away. Wheeler wondered at his miraculous recovery.

Colonel Richard Irving Dodge commanded all the infantry and artillery regiments that participated in the Powder River Expedition. Credit: Library of Congress

dinner: Bacon and Flap jacks. Not much running around today and
stade close to my tent nor had no words with this Sargent magor.

What Colonel Mackenzie thought of this fracas between Smith
and his sergeant is difficult to say, for he had heavier matters
weighing on his increasingly troubled mind. Crook's compli-
ments notwithstanding, Colonel Richard Dodge's assessment of the
battle, in no small part a product of the fierce competitiveness
and pettiness that plagued officer-officer relations on the frontier,
would not have surprised Mackenzie: "Altogether it has been a
very successful affair," Dodge confided to his diary, yet, he added,
"It might have been much more so had McKenzie [sic] possessed
as much administrative and political sagacity as he has gallantry
in the field. Still it is no time, nor is their [sic] any cause for
grumbling. The affair stamps our campaign as a success even if
nothing more is accomplished. I only regret that my portion of
the Command had no share or lot in the affair. All say that had
the Doboys been there not an Indian would have escaped. If I had
been allowed to go," the Colonel boasted, "we would have had a
more complete story to tell."[20]

However, when Colonel Mackenzie openly chastised himself for
failing to pursue the Cheyennes into the rocks behind the village,
Dodge responded with words of encouragement, emphasizing
Mackenzie's success. In a revealing account of Mackenzie's assessment of the battle and, sadly, an early sign of the colonel's growing
insanity, Dodge recorded the following in his journal:

> We found him [Mackenzie] very downcast—bitterly reproaching
> himself for what he called his failure. He talked more like a crazy
> man than the sane commander of a splendid body of Cavalry. He
> said to an officer that if he had courage enough he would blow his
> brains out. [The other officers present] went out soon, and Mac
> opened his heart to me. He is excessively sensitive. He said he had
> often done better with a third of the force at his command
> here—that he believed he degenerated as a soldier as he got
> older—that he regarded the whole thing as an utter failure. He
> even stated that he was sensitive lest someone might attribute cow-
> ardice to him—and much more of the same kind.

20. Dodge diary, Nov. 29, 1876, Newberry Library.

He was so worked up that he could hardly talk and had often to stop and collect himself. I bullied him and encouraged him all I could—told him that he was foolish and absurd to talk so, that we all regarded the affair as a grand success and that his record was too well known for anyone to attribute cowardice to him. I left him feeling much better, but he was in such a state that I thought it right to tell General Crook about it. The General was greatly worried and soon left my tent, I think to send for Mac and get him to play whist or something.[21]

The funeral for the five enlisted men had precipitated the commander's emotional crisis. Lieutenant John McKinney's body would be shipped back to home and family, but it was a final gesture underscoring the caste system of the frontier army that enlisted men received no such privilege. They were buried in the far off country where they had died. The funeral took place at noon on November 30 near the camp on Crazy Woman Creek. The service, in Dodge's estimation, was "most creditable. . . . All proper ceremonies and honors were paid, and the dead placed in their graves with the solemn words of the Episcopal service."[22] Lieutenant Homer Wheeler would later remember the funeral taking place on a "beautiful winter's morning" and, inaccurately, "in a beautiful wooded valley where Fort Reno had been some years before."[23] Lieutenant John Bourke provided his view of it in a later rendering of the mortuary service:

> There was no gorgeous ritual, no solemn chant, no peal of cathedral organ or sad refrain of cathedral bell, but more tenderly imposing than all these was the funeral procession of over six hundred weather-beaten veterans, headed by Generals George Crook, Ranald Mackenzie, Colonels Dodge, Townsend and Gordon, with all the members of their Staffs and the hundreds of savage auxiliaries—which moved with measured tread to the place of sepulture and there halted until the extracts of the Book of Common Prayer had been read.
>
> The usual funeral salute was fired, and then the bugles sang

21. Ibid., Nov. 30, 1876, Newberry Library.
22. Ibid.
23. Wheeler, *Frontier Trail*, 184–85.

"taps" and our heroes were left to sleep their last sleep un-
disturbed.[24]

How did the "weather-beaten veterans" perceive the funeral?
Offering the usual contrast between officer and enlisted man, they
saw it in less lyrical terms. Sergeant James McClellan, for example, simply noted in his diary: "at noon we had a funeral. all
the cavalry turned out mounted and armed. we buried five of the
men shot at the Powder river cannon fight. The officer is to be
taken east."[25] Private Smith, having been relieved of orderly duty
earlier that day, served as a pallbearer and mused a bit more on
the prospects of a wilderness grave:

Friday December 1st 1876[26]

I had not had my Brekfast long when my old friend [Sergeant
Major Walsh] come to me and sed the Genrell say you can Report
back to your company. I says all right. I node it was his dooings
becous I would not cook. Well this winds up my ordley carrer.

I went to my company and reported for dooty. I now expected
to git hell all a round for When a man is off a while they stick
every thing on to him that there is to do. But they yoused me poty
well this time. For I all ways tride to do right as near as I node how.

I had not been back long when the first Sargent come to me and
says you will bee one of the Pall Bors [pall bearers] at the funral
this afternoon. The Leut. in charge of our Company see me and
cald me up to him and says how is your horse Smith is he shod? I
seys all right, Leut. He say you will bee one of the 25 men out of
the Company to go out tonite to jump a nother Indin Camp. His
name was Leut. Shoomaker[27] and was a fine man to. He told me

24. Bourke, *Mackenzie's Last*, 44–45; Bourke diary, Nov. 30, 1876, Denver
Public Library, 1440–41.

25. McClellan Journal, Nov. 30, 1876, typescript.

26. Smith mistakenly recorded the funeral as occurring on Dec. 1, 1876. All
other diaries indicate the funeral took place on Nov. 30.

27. Frank Shoemaker, a Pennsylvanian, graduated from the U.S. Military
Academy at West Point in 1868 and soon after accepted a commission as second
lieutenant, 4th Cavalry. By the time of the Dull Knife Battle, he was 34 years
old and a first lieutenant. Shoemaker evidently did not relish frontier duty, for
his military service records indicate an eagerness to seek duty as instructor of
cavalry tactics at West Point or in the recruiting service. He also collected, in
Gen. William T. Sherman's words, "more than a fair share of 'leave.'" The

he was glad I was back in the Company. You see this name Smith was handey where ever I was.

In the afternoon we went to berrey the ded and it was the hardest looking funral I was ever at. Well, we goot done and went back. I jest thought then I would never like to bee left in the ground in this wild cuntry whear no white man would ever see the place a gane. The way they berrey in this cuntry they take and sow a man up in a Blanket and dont have no coffin.

We had not been back long when stable coll went and a Sargent in I Company went to the hird for his horse and little did he now it was his last time. For he had not more than goot on his horse then he fell with him and roled over him and he drod his last breath in about five minutes.[28] and this wound up the first day in our Company. I now went to bunking with a young fellow by the

---

lieutenant frequently requested leaves for not only his own sicknesses but those of his wife as well. In 1878, for example, he sought sick leave on account of rheumatism he contracted while on duty in the Department of the Platte during the winter of 1876–77 (the Powder River Expedition). After the decision had been made to have him examined by a medical board, Sherman in disgust wrote: "I want the Adjutant General in his rulings to enforce this decision. The United States employs an officer and pays him for all of his time. We are entitled to all his services be it that of a whole man—half-quarter & c. . . . Though habitually we can get along without the Rheumatic, yet sometimes we must have some of these. Even if their bodies be racked with pain. This officer . . . should be made to join his company at once." Lt. Shoemaker's willingness to use his family connections in order to achieve special privileges did not endear the officer to Sherman. His father was a judge, and his uncle a former Pennsylvania congressman. In addition, Pennsylvania's Gov. Henry Hoyt wrote a letter to Pres. Rutherford B. Hayes in 1879 urging Shoemaker's appointment as paymaster with the army and noting that the officer's family connections were "large & influential." Such connections apparently did not move Sherman, although Shoemaker was appointed captain in Nov. 1881. He resigned from the army June 30, 1883. Soon after giving notice, however, he changed his mind and tried to revoke his own resignation. Based on Mackenzie's recommendation, Sherman declined Shoemaker's attempts to regain his position. "I think he has behaved badly & there was no pressure brought by me on this officer to cause him to resign," Mackenzie reported. See Frank Shoemaker Military Service Record, File #3734 ACP 1871, Box 57, RG 94, NARS; Heitman, *Historical Register* 1:884.

28. Bourke identified him as Sgt. Patterson of Capt. Hemphill's company, 4th Cavalry. He was killed when his horse fell upon him and burst some of his anterior arteries. See Bourke diary, Dec. 1, 1876, Denver Public Library, 1441.

name of Deon[29] and we stade [together as bunkies] till spring
Broke us up.

The following day, Smith did not move out with a company of
twenty-four others "to jump another Indin camp." Only Luther
North and four others left the camp on Crazy Woman for sur-
veillance, and they found no sign of Indians.[30] Few knew Crook's
plans, for he did not even share them with Colonels Mackenzie
and Dodge, although the latter heard rumors of a move toward
Cantonment Reno:

> I was just going to Headquarters to inquire [about this] when I met
> Mackenzie who was coming to my tent. He also had heard some-
> thing of the move, but had no orders. While we were discussing
> the probabilities and rather pitching into Crook for his most ex-
> traordinary and unnecessary reticence, he came in. I asked him to
> sit, but he said "I've only a moment to stay." "You will march
> tomorrow and should make arrangements tonight for crossing the
> river." "What river?" I asked. "This," he replied. I said, "I have
> heard we are to march back to Reno. Is it so?" He said, "Yes." Just
> then Mackenzie made a motion as if to ask a question, when Crook
> abruptly left the tent without saying "By your leave, or D———m
> your soul, ar any such pleasantry" as the Irishman had it. Well all
> calculations are baffled.
>
> I went down to Headquarters tonight and enquired around to
> learn if any scouts are in—None that anyone knows of. It is not
> then a move founded on recent information. I conjecture that it is
> merely a change of base. Crook is satisfied that Crazy Horse has
> left Tongue river and gone into the bad lands around Slim Butte.
> We will probably strike for the Belle Fourche, with our base on the
> Black Hills. All right—I don't care particularly where we cam-
> paign—one place on these plains is about equal to another, and
> this new move will place us nearer to mail and friends. The only

29. This was probably Vachel Dean, a 25-year-old farmer from Terre Haute,
Ind. He had enlisted at St. Louis, Mo., the previous August. At the time of his
enlistment he was described as 5 feet, 6 and three-quarter inches tall, with gray
eyes, light-colored hair, and a ruddy complexion. Dean remained in the service
for his full 5-year enlistment and was discharged Aug. 2, 1881, from Fort Elliott,
Texas, as a sergeant. See "Register of Enlistments in the U.S. Army, 1798–
1914," NARS, M–233, 73:80.
30. North, *Man of the Plains*, 219.

serious point is that we are also nearer supplies and this move may materially lengthen our campaign.[31]

In a series of letters to General Sheridan from the camp on Crazy Woman's Fork, Crook laid out the plans he kept from his own officers. He believed that Mackenzie's fight would cause Crazy Horse and Sitting Bull to leave the Rosebud and Tongue River country. Sitting Bull would head north of the Yellowstone. Crazy Horse, Crook argued, would move toward the vicinity of Slim Buttes, "in which case it will be an impossibility for us to follow him." But, he added, "I shall endeavor to ascertain these points before leaving here, so that in case they leave the Rosebud country, I will not make that march as it would unfit the horses of the command for any further service this winter, and in case Crazy Horse has gone to Slim Buttes, I will go there via the Black Hills."[32]

Crook did not know the effect the Cheyennes' defeat on the Red Fork would have on other "hostile" Indians, but he was certain that the people of that village, without a vestige of clothing and "with starvation and perishing with cold starring [sic] them in the face," posed no further threat. He did not intend to pursue them.[33] Instead, he would move down the Little Powder and establish a temporary base near the center of the country where the Sioux and others who refused to surrender were likely to take refuge. Crook expected to apply pressure on them at least until the end of December—after which, he believed, it would not do to follow them, because the animals would be in poor condition and forage nearly gone. He was also convinced that whether or not this campaign settled the issue for all time, the Indians would never again be as formidable as they had been the previous summer.[34]

Meantime, Morning Star's destitute Northern Cheyennes fled the Big Horn Mountains in search of sanctuary among the Sioux.[35]

31. Dodge diary, Dec. 1, 1876, Newberry Library.
32. George Crook to Philip Sheridan, Nov. 30, 1876, copy contained in Powder River Expedition Order Book, John G. Bourke Papers, USMA.
33. Ibid.
34. George Crook to Philip Sheridan, Dec. 1, 1876, copy contained in Powder River Expedition Order Book, John G. Bourke Papers, USMA.
35. Marquis, *Wooden Leg*, 286.

Around November 28, several Cheyennes returned to the battle-
ground to see if any horses had escaped from army hands and
returned to the campsite. They found a good many had either
been left or returned on their own.[36] The sight of these horses
delighted the Cheyennes, although without saddles they had to
ride bareback. Traveling remained difficult moving from one
campfire to the next, stopping so that the weak ones, the women,
and the children, would not freeze to death. Yet even in a time of
such suffering, the Northern Cheyennes did not lose their sense
of humor, at least in retrospect. John Stands in Timber remembered that Wolf Tooth, along on that journey, acquired quite a
coat when he killed a buffalo and cut out the soft part of the hide
from the belly to cover his shoulders like a cloak. Placing a pin
through the hide at the neck and another down below, it kept him
warm. But it also froze stiff so that he could not remove it. "He
had to wear it," Stands in Timber dryly noted, "for a long time."[37]

After following the ridge of the Big Horns to the head of Clear
Creek, the fugitives traveled the course of that stream to Lake De
Smet. Then they crossed over to the head of Prairie Dog Creek,
adhering to it until they came upon the Tongue River. From the
Tongue they went up Otter Creek and crossed over to Beaver
Creek, where, eleven days after the battle, they found Crazy
Horse's camp.[38] The Oglalas treated them hospitably, sharing their
food, blankets, robes, tobacco, and even their horses. Every married woman received enough skins to make a lodge for her house-
hold.[39] After resting a few days, the chiefs of both tribes held a
council and decided to travel and hunt together for a time, at least
until the Cheyennes replenished their supply of buffalo meat and
skins.[40]

While the Northern Cheyennes found their way to friends, Pri-

36. Grinnell, *Fighting Cheyennes*, 382; John Stands in Timber maintained
that after the soldiers left the battlefield, the Cheyennes decided there was no
point in returning to the village site. See Stands in Timber, *Cheyenne Memories*,
218.
37. Stands in Timber, *Cheyenne Memories*, 219.
38. Grinnell, *Fighting Cheyennes*, 382.
39. Stands in Timber, *Cheyenne Memories*, 218; Marquis, *Wooden Leg*,
287–88.
40. Marquis, *Wooden Leg*, 288–89.

vate Smith found his way back to Cantonment Reno and what he
hoped was the first step toward an end to this winter campaign.

Saturday Dec. 2nd

Broke camp about 9 oclock and marched 28 mils on the back trail and
camped on Powder River about 1 mile from old Fort Reno. I was
poot on gard hear for the first time in a long while and I node we
were hedding for home.

On this matter, he was sorely mistaken. The Powder River
country would not yet loosen its hold on Smith and the others of
his column. Some of the hardest aspects of a winter campaign still
lay before them.

CHAPTER 6

Crook's Campaign Concludes

Private Smith was not the only one uncertain of General George Crook's plans for the Powder River Expedition. Some wagered the general would head up the Belle Fourche River, toward the Black Hills and a clash with Crazy Horse. Others simply hoped he would end the winter campaign.[1] As enlisted men debated their immediate fates, disgruntled officers did the same. None was more perturbed about the uncertainty, secrecy, and doubt than Lieutenant Colonel Richard Dodge. On December 2, Crook had informed him they would remain at Cantonment Reno through the next day. Yet, on December 3, one of Crook's orderlies roused Dodge out of bed with orders to get his command off as soon as possible. "I was disgusted," Dodge complained in his journal, "but there is no use in being so with Crook's orders. He really does not know ahead what he intends to do. Makes up his mind at the last moment, and then acts at once—expecting everybody else to do the same."[2]

That was also the day when the Shoshone scouts took their

---

1. For an example, see Sgt. James McClellan's Journal, Dec. 2, 1876, typescript copy loaned to author by Thomas R. Buecker, Fort Robinson Historic Site, Nebr.

2. Dodge diary, Dec. 2 and 3, 1876, Newberry Library.

leave of the command, heading west to their homes near Wyoming's Wind River Mountains.[3] After discovering evidence in Morning Star's village that some of their own people had been recently attacked and killed, the Shoshones applied for release from scouting duties and Crook consented.[4] "Our parting with them," Lieutenant John Bourke later wrote, "was such as would take place between brothers bound together by the ties of dangers conquered and elements defied together."[5] In his diary he recorded their ceremonial good-byes:

> The Shoshones drew up in line of battle, as if on parade, and then Cosgrove[6] told us they wanted to give General Crook, Capt. Pollock, Lt. [Walter] Schuyler and myself a few testimonials of regard before setting out to rejoin their own people. These were all articles taken from the hostiles and very curious in workmanship.
>
> To General Crook they gave a stone pipe. To Captain Pollock a "medicine shirt," as it is called, of buckskin painted black and fringed with scalp-locks and yellow horse-hair plumes taken presumably from the helmets of soldiers of the ill-fated 7th Cavalry. On the ground before Schuyler and self they laid a bow and quiver full of vicious looking arrows of unusual size, a saddle cover of buckskin embroidered in beadwork, a bed cover or something of that sort, adorned in much the same way, a pair of heavily ornamented mocassins, and a war shield of grotesque workmanship, circular in form and protected in front by a thick coating of eagle and other feathers, difficult for a bullet to penetrate. . . . [7]

3. The other Indian scouts would remain with the Powder River Expedition until it reached Fort Fetterman at the end of December.

4. George Crook to Capt. John Mise, Dec. 2, 1876, copy contained in Powder River Expedition Order Book, John G. Bourke Papers, USMA.

5. Bourke, *Mackenzie's Last*, 45.

6. Tom Cosgrove was in principal charge of the Shoshone scouts who participated in the Powder River Expedition. He was a Texas native who served as captain of a company in the 32d Texas Cavalry, Confederate States of America. After the Civil War he moved to the Northwest and had served as scout along with Shoshones earlier in 1876, participating in the Battle of the Rosebud on June 17. He died in 1877. See a brief biographical statement and photo of Cosgrove in "A Day With the 'Fighting Cheyennes,'" *Motor Travel Magazine* (May 1930): 19.

7. Bourke diary, Dec. 3, 1876, Denver Public Library, 1442–43.

Through December 4 and 5 the soldiers and remaining scouts stayed put. Still Crook told no one of his plans, and still Dodge remained convinced he had none. "I am sorry to say," he groused, "that I do not believe he has any definite plan or expectation. He proposes to go a certain distance in a certain direction hoping like Mr. Macawber that something may turn up, but his actions convince me that he either has no plan, or that it is very illy made."[8]

Others became equally annoyed. After observing Mackenzie's command strike their tents and saddle their horses, Luther North and the Pawnees followed suit. They assumed all would move. Then came word they would not march after all. Two days in a row this happened. On the third day, December 6, North and the Pawnees refused to take down their tents until General Crook himself pulled out. "I never saw such an outfit in my life," Frank North griped. "Nobody knows five minutes beforehand what is to be done."[9]

Finally, on December 5, an exasperated Colonel Dodge pointedly asked Crook his plans:

... I told him that I did not ask out of mere curiosity but that if there was no reason for secrecy I wanted to know what were his plans for the next thirty days. To my surprise and pleasure he said there was no secrecy at all, and that he would tell me all I wanted to know. I got the maps and went for him with a lot of questions.

We are to march by Pumpkin Buttes to the Belle Fourche and go down that stream to its Forks—then strike across to Little Powder river and continue down that to its junction with Big Powder. From there as a center the Indians [scouts] will radiate in all directions. If they find a village we will go for it on packmules. If not we will return.

I carefully estimated the distances with him. "It will take," I said, "about ten days for the Command to reach that point. Allow two days for the Indians to report and it will be, say, the 18th of this month before we commence our Pack mule march. Suppose that to last ten days we will get back to our wagons by the 28th. With the utmost expedition we cannot get back to this camp under 6 days—or by 3d January. We have rations only to the 31 Dec. Now

8. Dodge diary, Dec. 4, 1876, Newberry Library.
9. North, *Man of the Plains*, 220.

how can you manage it?" He said, "I want to be back to this Camp by the 28th of this month, and to Fort Fetterman by 31st. If we should strike Indians while on packmule scout anywhere within two or three days march of the mouth of Tongue River, we will go in there and get some rations. If we don't find a village we will come back without the packmule scout." [10]

Of these plans, Private Smith knew nothing. His return to Company E, Fourth Cavalry, meant he no longer kept the company of generals and colonels. It is doubtful he cared. But if his terse diary entries from December 3 on are any indication of mood and disposition, he was none too happy about the turn of events. More of winter in Wyoming lay ahead for this soldier. Only the sick and wounded were released from further campaign duty:

Sunday Dec. 3rd 1876

Left camp [on the Powder River near Cantonment Reno] earley and made 15 miles and went into camp on dry Fork and this was bad Watter. Very muddy and not much of it.

Monday Dec. 4th 1876

Lay over hear to day and all the wounded and all the sick and men with the worst horses left us and started for Fort Fetterman and hear they lay the Sargent of I Company under the ground.

Tuesday Dec. 5th 1876

Struck camp and did not moove after all, so I carred wood a gane all day went on hed quarter gard and goot a good super there from the nigor.

Finally, on December 6 the troops received word to break camp:

Wensday Dec. 6th 1876

Laeft camp and a bout noon and made 15 mils and camped on some wotter holes the grass was pooty good here weather fine.[11]

10. Dodge diary, Dec. 5, 1876, Newberry Library.
11. Lt. Col. Dodge found both the grass and the water quite good at this camping spot: "At 2:30 p.m. after a long detour to the south east, we suddenly turned to the north and soon after came to camp in a ravine running a little north of west, in which was a spring of water deep and clear and only slightly alkaline—much better than any we have had for some time past. Better even

Thirsday Dec. 7th 1876

Broke camp earley and made 20 mils and went into camp on some wotter holes pased some miners on the road going to ded Wood [Deadwood] city.[12]

Luther North urged these miners to turn back because of the state of the Indian war in that country. But they ignored his advice. Several days later one of the miners came straggling into the army camp, half crazed and half frozen, with the news that his party had been attacked. North and others went out to search for the rest and, upon reaching their campsite, discovered that one of the miners had been killed and all of their provisions and bedding, and all but one of their horses were stolen.[13]

This event prompted Colonel Dodge to offer his private views on the frontiersman—the valiant pioneer—whom he found himself compelled, by military duty, to protect. Dodge's view was none too positive, but quite typical of many army officers who served in the trans-Mississippi West:[14]

> The fate of this man, and the party, illustrates a peculiar phase of character of the large majority of the men who risk their lives on the frontier, mining, trapping, or prospecting. They are brave to imbecility or stupid beyond expression. A few men, possibly comparative strangers to each other, band together and agree to go to this or that place. Without apparently the slightest concern, they plunge into unknown wilderness, and through countries swarming with treacherous and deadly Indians. They travel without order and without care. If while hunting one should discover Indians, he rushes back to his party, which flies if it can, or fights with courage and tenacity if necessary. Arrived at a camping place they turn out their stock, get supper and go to bed, unconcerned as if no danger

---

than Powder or Crazy Woman. There is also very good and abundant grass, but no wood." See Dodge diary, Dec. 6, 1876, Newberry Library.

12. Luther North believed these miners were on their way to the Big Horn Mountains (*Man of the Plains*, 221). Dodge reported they were on their way to Montana from the Black Hills (Dodge diary, Dec. 7, 1876, Newberry Library).

13. George Crook to Chief Quartermaster, Dec. 13, 1876, copy contained in Powder River Expedition Order Book, USMA; North, *Man of the Plains*, 221. George Bird Grinnell maintains that Sioux, not Cheyennes, attacked this party of miners (*Fighting Cheyennes*, 369).

14. See Smith, "'Civilization's Guardians,'" 219–28.

were around them. If jumped they have no chance and lose all, and as in this case—were we not here by the merest chance for them, not one would likely escape alive.

I once when travelling with a train and troops, came on the high wide prairie suddenly on the form of a man, lying on his stomach and sleeping profoundly. He was at least 30 miles from any road and in a very dangerous country. I called to him loudly. He sat up and gazed stupidly for a moment or two then smiled and seemed relieved. "Where do you belong," I asked. "I come from Iowa," he answered. "What are you doing here?" I demanded very peremptorily. "Oh, I am looking for work," he said genially. I thought at first that he was a lunatic, but further questioning satisfied me that he was only an ordinary plain lunatic, that is, one who feared no danger because he saw none.[15]

If Private Smith heard of the miners' fate he did not record his reaction in his diary. Instead, he carried on with his increasingly humdrum account of the campaign's closing days:

Friday Dec. 8th 1876

Laeft camp earley and made 18 mils and camped on Sage crick.[16] No wood hear nothing but sage brush. Very cold was on gard.

Saturday Dec. 9th 1876

Broke camp as yousel [usual] and made 8 mils and camped on hed waters of Belle Fourche. There was lots of cotton wood to bee cut hear for the horses.

Sunday Dec. 10th 1876

Moved camp down the crick about 8 mils and struck a nice camp the best we had been at in a long time lots of wood and wotter. A large train left the command to go to Fort Fetemon for suplyes. The command was strung along this crick for 2 or 3 mils the command was strung along this crick for 2 or 3 mils.

Monday Dec. 11th 1876

Lay over all day and it was a fine day.

Tuesday Dec. 12th 1876

Still we lay over and fearful windy and cold.

15. Dodge diary, Dec. 11, 1876, Newberry Library.
16. McClellan and Dodge identify the camp as on the Belle Fourche.

Wensday Dec. 13th 1876

Moved camp 3 or 4 miles farther down the crick.

Thirsday Dec. 14th 1876

Lay over all day and the weather was fine.

Friday Dec. 15th 1876

I awok in the morning and found, to my surprise that I had no hoss for the hird had stampeded durring the nite. I never saw the men in as good yoummer [humor] as they were this morning every boddy praying that they would never find them for we had been worked to death cutting cotton wood for them. I Company was ordered out to look for them and brought them back towards nite. Lay over to day.

After the excitement of the campaign's early days, marching up the Bozeman Trail and engaging the enemy in combat, these post-battle days must have seemed uneventful. In addition, Bourke commented, that "there was about the winter scenery of that part of Wyoming a bleak and barren dreariness, whose montony at times appalled the traveller conscious of its magnitude. . . . The leaden pall of the cloudy sky was an effective setting for the cheerless landscape which, in spite of its gloom, had still a weird fascination over the sight which never tired of looking at it."[17] Nearly every day, the officer claimed, a fierce blizzard pummelled the troops and nearly every night they camped in a spot where water was scarce, alkaline and muddy. At one spot they had to use water from a hole "swarming with wriggling worms."[18] To make matters even worse, fuel was scarce, with greasewood and sagebrush often serving as the best available. But the major problem was lack of forage for the horses, since the ground was snow-covered and the grass not accessible. Horses and mules had to settle for half-rations, just at a time when they needed more food to maintain their physical stamina.[19]

Colonel Dodge did not allow this forage problem to go unnoticed in his running commentary-criticism of the commanding officer:

17. Bourke, *Mackenzie's Last*, 53.
18. Ibid., 45. See also Dodge diary, Dec. 26, 1876, Newberry Library.
19. Bourke, *Mackenzie's Last*, 47.

However good a soldier Crook may be, he has no administrative ability whatever. He well knows that this part of the expedition must be a failure, if for no other reason, because we cannot transport our supplies. His train is in wretched condition, yet he does nothing to get or keep it in order. He might be a cavalryman, for his carelessness of his means of transportation. Mules are the very first element of success in such an expedition as this. Yet he seems to care nothing whatever for his mules. The Cavalry horses and Indian ponies are giving out every day, and by the time we reach the mouth of Little Powder, it will be a miracle if more than half of us do not have to walk back. Yet he pushes on. I would not say it out loud—but I think he is pushing on now simply from vanity. It will look well to go on—no matter at what cost of life or property. He will come to great grief someday, for this trait of character. . . .

He is no doubt a good indoor Quartermaster, but he leaves the whole management of his train to understrappers, who neglect it entirely. No mule is ever curried—some of them are cruelly beaten—they get no grazing because he is too tender with his teamsters to make them go on herd. Altogether the transportation of this expedition is the very worst managed I have ever seen and if for no other reason the expedition must be a failure.

I find there is no sort of use in talking to Crook and it really seems sometimes as if he expected a failure, and intended to lay the blame on the failure of his means of transportation. You might just as well go in now, but his pride will make him kill a few hundred animals first.[20]

If the horses and mules lacked sufficient food, the same could not be said of the officers. Along with fresh elk and antelope, they discovered that the Indian scouts willingly shared ideas about cuisine, and the adventuresome Lieutenant Bourke, at least, found their dishes quite palatable, pronouncing elk heart boiled in salt

20. Dodge diary, Dec. 7 and 8, 1876, Newberry Library. Gen. William T. Sherman agreed that Crook's management of provisions was less than perfect. He believed that Crook was empowered to obtain whatever he needed for his troops. "If his men were not properly provided with everything," Sherman wrote Philip Sheridan, "it was his own fault." William Sherman to Philip Sheridan, Feb. 2, 1877, Box 17, RG 393, Division of the Missouri, Special File, Sioux War 1876, NARS.

General George Crook, commander of the Powder River Expedition, during the Black Hills Campaign, 1875–1876. Credit: Wyoming State Archives, Museums and Historical Department

water as "good enough for anybody" and antelope liver, sliced thin and roasted over hot coals on both sides, "extremely appetizing." He also found deer or antelope head roasted in ashes "toothsome," buffalo entrails "savory and palatable," and fresh elk liver not unlike raw oysters.[21] But even this courageous soul would have drawn the line of "scientific enthusiasm" as he reported in his diary that Colonel Dodge did:

> Colonel Dodge told us yesterday that one of the Pawnees had approached him with something in his handerchief, telling him it was "heap good." An examination showed [it was] the granulated liver of an elk chased for so long a time before being killed that it had lost the semblance of itself and had turned into big clots of blood. Over this had been sprinkled the gall of the animal and of this bloody, greenish looking mixture, the fastidious Colonel was invited to partake. He felt compelled to decline. [The Pawnee] looked at him with an air of compassion and then swallowed the mess himself, leaving nothing but the dirty handerchief.[22]

Bourke's relative open-mindedness about the Indians' customs found its limits not only in granulated elk liver but also in their forms of entertainment. The scouts, he complained, did not wait for invitations to serenade the camp every night. Instead, the Sioux serenaded and danced for the Pawnees one night and the Pawnees returned the favor the next: "Ditto the whole business for the Arapahoes; ditto for the Cheyennes. Then the Arapahoes, fired by enthusiasm, went over the whole programme with the Sioux and we had to endure another round of dittoes." Nobody growled about that, he maintained, because all understood these were common ceremonial observances. The limits to his patience were reached, however, "just as we were getting ready for a real good honest sleep, [when] the Pawnees started in on a Farewell Tour; the Sioux not to be outdone, and 'in deference to the urgent request of many patrons, kindly consented to appear for this night only,' and the Arapahoes 'yielding to the importunate demands of a clamorous public had cancelled important European engagements in order to etc. etc. etc.' We managed to live through it all.

21. Bourke, *Mackenzie's Last*, 48.
22. Bourke diary, Dec. 11, 1876, Denver Public Library, 1480.

It was a very gloomy season in our lives, one I would gladly bury in oblivion." [23]

Unfortunately, the scouts did not leave written records of their impressions concerning the soldiers' cuisine (mostly hardtack) or their "civilized" forms of entertainment, which on this expedition consisted largely of drinking and gambling. Colonel Dodge, for one, did attempt to curb the whiskey trade, and its consequent disorder, by issuing a special order on December 15 that forbade the sutler from selling liquor to anyone but commissioned officers. The officers, then, could distribute the alcohol to their men and assume responsibility for their behavior. [24] On December 16, when he realized the company commanders failed to respond to this plan, Dodge revoked the order and allowed the sutler to sell liquor by the drink to enlisted men under the condition that they not be already inebriated. [25] Of all this, Private Smith wrote:

Saturday Dec. 16th 1876

Lay over today and some of the boys goot drunk at the sutler's. Lots of them. Whiskey only one dollar a drink. It was pooty hard for me to keep a way from this now for I had mad lots of money renting my tent out at nite to fellows to gamble in. One nite I goot 10 dollars from one fellow. He had won 1000 dollars. I had quite a good stake saved up now. Over 40 dollars I had saved in this way.

Sunday Dec. 17th 1876

Worked hard all fore noon, choping cotton wood. The suply trane came back today. [26] A fine day.

23. Bourke, *Mackenzie's Last*, 48.

24. Special Order No. 21, Headquarters Artillery and Infantry Battalions, Powder River Expedition, Dec. 15, 1876, Entry 3962, Vol. 1, RG 393, Powder River Expedition, Letters Received, NARS. In his diary, Dodge noted that Crook paid him a visit that day: "His object in coming was that I should not be too stringent on the Sutler." See Dodge diary, Dec. 15, 1876, Newberry Library.

25. Special Order No. 22, Headquarters Artillery and Infantry Battalions, Powder River Expedition, Dec. 16, 1876, Entry 3962, Vol. 1, RG 393, Powder River Expedition Letters Received, NARS.

26. According to Lt. Col. Dodge, this train consisted of 80 wagons, 128,000 pounds of forage, and 12 half-day rations for the men. See Dodge diary, Dec. 17, 1876, Newberry Library.

Monday Dec. 18th 1876

This day there was most all the Sargents and Corprals goot fearful drunk and a privite by the name of Moore[27] was drunk and was poot under gard. When we were after the hird at stable call Moore had to go also. He could not untie a [k]not [that] was in his holter, for it was one sollid lump of ice. The first Sargent ran up to him and gave him an affle kick and a welt in the fase. He did not say a word back and neather did the sentry.

When we led up to the Picket line Moore asked the sentry to let him go to the tent for his currie come [comb] and Brush, Witch he did. When he come out he had his pistell in his right hand behind him and the sentry did not see it. When the first Sargent come along the man that struck him at the crick he pooled down on him with the Pistell and as luck or bad luck would have it, it mist fire, and he snaped down on three catcherrigs [cartridges] and none of them went off.

By this time the boys had grabed him and goot the Pistell a way from him. And then the Sargent ran up and punched him in the fase when they held him. They now tide him up to a wagon. The Leut. told me to take a rope and help to tie him up. I picked up the rope and walked over to the wagon and throde it down and walked a round the wagon. The sentry goot [put] under gard to. Nothing else sed to any body else drunk.

Such scuffles were, unfortunately, common. Only a few days before, a general court-martial was convened to hear charges against Corporal Michael Cooney and Private John Kennard, both of Company K, Fourth Artillery. Private Kennard not only failed to obey Cooney's orders to place some stoves on a wagon, but had used disrespectful and insubordinate language to boot—something to the effect of "God damn it, do you take me for a damn fool?" At this point, the corporal assaulted Kennard with a campstool, retorting, "God damn you, call me a damn fool, will you?" Both corporal and private pled guilty to the charges.

27. This was probably John Moore, a railroadman from Huntington, Pa., who enlisted in the army Jan. 7, 1876, at Pittsburgh, Pa. He was about 22 years old during the Powder River Expedition. Moore had brown eyes, brown hair, a fair complexion, and stood 5 feet, 5 and three-quarters inches tall. The army and Moore apparently did not agree, for on Jan. 7, 1877, 1 year exactly after his original enlistment, the young private deserted. The treatment Moore received from the sergeant that Smith describes may explain his desertion. See "Register of Enlistments in the U.S. Army, 1798–1915," M–233, Roll 39, 75:104, NARS.

Cooney's sentence consisted of a reprimand by his company commander—a light sentence on account of previous good character. Kennard, apparently, did not have the same reputation (and he certainly did not have the rank), for his sentence came to confinement at hard labor for three months and forfeiture of thirty dollars of his pay to the United States government.[28]

Commissioned officers were not above such quarrels either. About one month earlier, Lieutenant Greenough and Captain J. B. Campbell, also of the Fourth Artillery, flung charge and counter-charge at one another. According to Greenough, the captain was guilty of mimicking his gait while the lieutenant limped along at the head of his company. Adding insult to injury, Campbell did this in the presence of other officers and enlisted men. Furthermore, he charged, Campbell was drunk in the officers' clubroom at Fort Fetterman. In response, the captain pointed out to General Crook that Greenough preferred these charges against him only after he had first charged the lieutenant with insubordination and disrespectful behavior, thus giving the charges an appearance of retaliation. Colonel Dodge concurred with this view. Crook did too, and so, informed Lieutenant Greenough his charges against Captain Campbell would not be entertained.[29] All of these court-martial matters severely taxed Dodge's patience, particularly those

28. General Orders No. 2, Dec. 15, 1876, copy contained in Powder River Expedition Order Book, John G. Bourke Papers, United States Military Academy Library, West Point. In other court-martial proceedings, Pvt. Charles F. Smith, Company D, 14th Infantry, was charged with straggling from the ranks and using insubordinate language when addressing an officer on the march from Crazy Woman Creek to Willow Creek, Nov. 26. When he was arrested, Smith refused to go with the guard. Smith pled guilty and was sentenced to 6 months' hard labor and fined $10 per month during that period. The court advised leniency "on account of his manifest ignorance displayed before the Court." See General Order No. 4, Dec. 19, 1876, copy contained in Powder River Expedition Order Book. USMA. Musician William Lally, Company G, 14th Infantry, was found guilty of calling Sgt. Francis M. Washburn a liar while camped at Crazy Woman's Fork, Dec. 1, 1876. Furthermore, when Lally was confined by the sergeant for this offense, the musician told him, "I'll kill you, you black son of a bitch." While Lally pled guilty to the first offense and innocent to the second, the Court found him guilty on both counts. He was sentenced to confinement under guard for 2 months and a $20 fine. See General Orders No. 4, Dec. 19, 1876, Powder River Expedition Order Book, John G. Bourke Papers, USMA.

29. The details of this conflict can be found in Powder River Expedition Order Book, John G. Bourke Papers, UMSA, 34, 39.

courts convened for the smallest and most inconsequential of of-
fenses. He thought it absurd, in fact, to try officers "for every little
offense. It only hardens them and renders them careless of any
blame of being before a court."[30]

Nevertheless, such problems as sutlers selling whiskey and officers offending one another preoccupied the troopers awaiting
word from Crook's spies and scouts of the enemies' whereabouts.
The waiting especially exasperated Crook, who informed Dodge
that he would not risk roaming around the country with the entire
command and that, if scouts did not return soon, he would end
the expedition. That was good news to Dodge, who offered a rare
note of praise for his commander. "I think he takes a very sensible
view of all the facts, and I expect I have done him injustice in
thought."[31] Such charity was short-lived, however, for several days
later Dodge returned to his customary assessment: "No one
knows what are the plans of General Crook. I don't believe he has
any, but expects to make up his mind when he gets further information. He is a regular bull-dog to hold on, and will not quit
unless forced to."[32]

Smith, in comparison, seemed almost serene in the midst of
the uncertainty. He neither fretted nor stewed about much of anything for several days:

Tuesday Dec. 19th 1876

Moved two or three mils down the crick. Weather mity fine today.

Wensday Dec. 20th 1876

Lay over all day and done nothing much.

Thirsday Dec. 21st 1876

Lay over all day and coot [cut] cotton wood. Weather fine. Every
thing quiet today.

What he did not realize was that on the twenty-first, General
Crook had given up on his scouts and spies and decided to end
the expedition. Both Dodge and Mackenzie agreed with Crook's
decision to conclude the campaign. So, the commanding officer of

30. Dodge diary, Dec. 14, 1876, Newberry Library.
31. Ibid., Dec. 13, 1876.
32. Ibid., Dec. 18, 1876.

the Powder River Expedition dashed off a telegram to Sheridan from the camp on the Belle Fourche:

> Recent operations have so stirred up the Indians that it is useless to try to catch them with the Command. The wornout condition of all the citizen and army transportation in this part of the Country makes it an impossibility to keep this command in the field any longer. Will arrive there in about six (6) days. After Indians settle and get over their shyness, a smaller command can be sent out with good prospect of catching them. The artillery can be spared if it is your desire to return it to the Pacific Coast. Please have full instructions for me at Fetterman on my arrival there.[33]

That night Colonels Dodge and Mackenzie learned the general was feeling rather low. Dodge thought it best to leave him alone, but Mackenzie argued Crook needed some consolation. "I could hardly keep from smiling at this," Dodge confessed, "for they were almost the identical words used by Crook to me when I told him how downhearted Mackenzie was after his fight."[34]

Once word had reached the ranks that the campaign was nearing its end, few—if any—shared Crook's depression. Most, in fact, were euphoric. Private Smith was certainly pleased. None knew, of course, that some of the severest weather the soldiers would face on this expedition still lay ahead:

Friday Dec. 22nd 1876

Broke camp at day brake and marched 15 mils and every body feeling good. We were on our back trale and Word went a round that we were a going in off of the Scout, snowing all day and cold.

Saturday Dec. 23rd 1876

The bugle sounded at 5 Oclock and we up and frose stiff. We mad 15 mils and camped on some wotter hols and not a stick of wood and the coldest day we had on the trip. I was now detailed for gard and I never shall forget it in all my life.

Sunday Dec. 24th 1876

Well morning came at last yes at last and I was never as glad to see a morning in all my life for such a nite as I had poot in. I had

33. George Crook to Philip Sheridan, Dec. 21, 1876, Box 17, RG 393, Division of the Missouri, Special File, Sioux War 1876, NARS.
34. Dodge diary, Dec. 21, 1876, Newberry Library.

to keep awake to keep from freesing to death. Corpral Hall[35] was in charge of the gard and I can all ways see him sitting by that sage Brush fire a bout as big as a wash pan with five blankets raped [wrapped] around him. When I walked my two ours-[hours] I run all the time and a round and a round I went and never stoped till my time was up. I was now pooty warm and thought I could sleep. I lade down with 14 Blankets over me and a lot under me but it would not work for I frose out and had to git out and pool Sage Bruch and run a round.

We left camp as yousel and made 12 mils and camped on Sage crick, and there was no wood hear neather but I had a stove in the tent and I and my Bunkey Pooled Sage Brush a nuff to keep warm with. This nite the thormometer was frose up and they could not tell how cold it was [but it was] the same the nite before this Nite. I went over to the commeiceres [commissary] and bought one can of Peaches. I gave 2 dollars for a can. I saw one man give 10 dollars for a bottle of Whiskey. I eate the Peaches. Crismas [Christmas] love. My bunkey helped.

"If I boasted that the hardships of a winter campaign were bearable," Dodge wrote, "I apologize. . . . This has been a day of terrible hardship and trial for all of us—men and animals."[36] His thermometer registered twenty degrees below zero before it froze and the general estimate of the lowest temperature ranged from thirty to forty degrees below. None of the soldiers died from exposure, but several mules did. Lieutenant Homer Wheeler later recalled one poor animal's demise. The mule insisted on backing into the tent that Wheeler occupied with Army Surgeon Marshal W. Wood, and everytime he did so, he loosened the tent cords. Several times during the night Wheeler trudged out to drive the mule away and tighten the cords. Once or twice he asked the surgeon to take a turn, but the doctor refused even though Wheeler warned him the tent might collapse on them if the mule persisted. His response: "Let her come!" Shortly after, it did. The dead mule, frozen stiff, fell upon the tent and nearly "came within

35. Cpl. David Hall enlisted in the army in April 1872 and was discharged from service in April 1877. See Muster Rolls, Company E, 4th Cavalry, Box 968, RG 94, Records of the Adjutant General's Office, NARS.
36. Dodge diary, Dec. 23, 1876, Newberry Library.

an ace of falling on the doctor, and from the state of my feelings at the time, I rather wished he had." [37] Both men spent an uncomfortable remainder of the night.

This Christmas, then, brought little joy to either officer or enlisted man. On Christmas Eve, while Smith ate his peaches, Crook invited several officers to his tent for a hot brandy punch. But the supply did not last long, and these more-privileged men scurried off to their cold beds. "Take it all in all it is a Xmas long to be remembered, and I don't care ever to have another like it," Dodge wrote. [38] Bourke agreed:

> One of the most disagreeable days in my experience was Christmas, 1876. We were pushing across the Pumpkin Buttes, doing our best to get into bivouac and escape the fury of the elements, which seemed eager to devour us. Beards, moustaches, eye-lashes and eye-brows were frozen masses of ice. The keen air was filled with minute crystals, each cutting the tender skin like a razor, while feet and hands ached as if beaten with clubs. Horses and mules shivered while they stood in column, their flanks white with crystals of perspiration congealed on their bodies, and their nostrils bristling with icicles. [39]

Private Smith described the day this way:

Monday Dec. 25th 1876

> Left camp as yousel and spent my Crismas on the road. Walked nearley all day. Made 20 mils and camped on some wotter holls. no wood. We had a reglar Old Crismas Dinner. A little peace of fat bacon and hard tack and a half a cup of coffee. You bet I thought of home now if ever I did. But fate was a gane me and I could not bee there. My Bunkey bought some candy and we ate it.

Next day, the troopers struck the old, familiar Bozeman Trail and headed south toward Fort Fetterman: [40]

37. Wheeler, *Frontier Trail*, 191.
38. Dodge diary, Dec. 25, 1876, Newberry Library.
39. Bourke, *Mackenzie's Last*, 53.
40. On reaching the Bozeman Trail, Dodge noted, "It was like an old friend and all hailed it with satisfaction." See Dodge diary, Dec. 26, 1876, Newberry Library.

Tuesday Dec. 26th 1876

Left our camp at Pumpkins Butes and made 12 mils and camped at our old camp on Wind River. Cut cotton wood till a way after dark.

Wensday Dec. 27th 1876

Laeft camp at 9 Oclock and made 17 mils and went into camp on South Fork of Cheyenne River. Plenty of wood hear. Snod all day.

Thirsday Dec. 28th 1876

Broke camp and [made] 13 mils and camped on Sage crick and mity cold. No wood and plenty of sage Brich to birn.[41]

Friday Dec. 29th 1876

Broke camp and marched 19 mils and camped 1 mile from Fort Feterman.

As the Powder River Expedition wound down to its final days, Ranald Mackenzie confided to Richard Dodge that this campaign had been a success after all, with little suffering. Regarding suffering, Dodge disagreed and openly said so, although he thought only of the white men's suffering and not the Northern Cheyennes'. To the point about the campaign's success, the lieutenant colonel also took exception, but kept such thoughts to himself. That evening Dodge mused in his diary about the meaning of success—thoughts prompted not only by Mackenzie's words, but by a letter he had received from his parents wherein they expressed their hopes that he would distinguish himself in service, yet risk no danger. The missive, he claimed,

> did me a world of good and reconciled me somewhat to going home without any special glory. The world applauds success— while success is an accident that may come to the stupid and unenergetic, as well as to the brightest and hardest worker. The world applauds success, but conscience approves him who does his work to the best of his ability whether he be successful or not. Neither myself nor my Command have done anything brilliant, but we have done our very best and had our luck put us in a fight, we

41. Dodge thought the temperature reached 25 degrees below zero before morning. See Dodge diary, Dec. 28, 1876, Newberry Library.

would have made a name for ourselves—or I am mighty mistaken. That's all![42]

With such matters, Private Smith had no apparent concern. Fame, fortune, success, or failure—these things mattered to ambitious officers. For the common soldier, mere survival and a good supper sufficed. This campaign had demonstrated that such simple hopes were not always met. Nor was there opportunity for a well-deserved rest. One day after reaching Fort Fetterman, Mackenzie and the cavalrymen moved on toward Camp Robinson:

Saturday Dec. 30th 1876

Left campin a hurrey this morning. Snow storm lasted all day. The road was fool of Straglers all day in all sort of ways. Nearley every Boddy drunk. We went in to camp after marching 18 mils. Now the next thing was supper but where was the cook wagon? It had tiped over and the teamster and quarter master sargents were drunk. Everything was in a grate growl and we had to go to bed with out any supper mitty hard luck.

Sunday Dec. 31st 1876

Laeft camp at the yousel time and marched 15 mils and camped on Elk Horn Crick. The boys in my tent were on gard and they made a raid on a whiskey wagon that was near. Some of the boys goot tide up to wagons. The boys in my tent came in some time in the nite and wooke me up and they had a coffe pot fool of whiskey and they would have me to take some. I took my tin cup and fild it and set it to my hed and told them I would drink it in the morning. I went to sleep and in the morning I found the cup all right. I did not titch it and went and bilt a fire in the stove. I now looked out and the Bugle had not gone yet. I looked down at my feet and hear I saw my Bunkey covered with snow. I pooled him in to the tent and bilt a big fire and after a while he come to. He was near frose to death. I now goot my cup of whiskey and gave it to him. Well he soon goot all right after drinking a quart of whiskey. I told him if I would of drank it [the whiskey] would of cild me and he says it jest saved my life. Well the Leut. when he found out how the whiskey had worked the company, he took

42. Dodge diary, Dec. 26, 1876, Newberry Library.

a[n] ax and stove in the heds of the kegs and let all the Poison run a way. And I for one was glad of it. But a grate meny gave a loud sye [sigh].

About one half of the company was under gard this day [presumably for drunkenness] and had to walk threw snow nee [knee] deep and so ended the last day of the year 1876.[43]

Monday January 1st, 1877

Laeft camp and marched 10 mils and went into camp on horse shooe crick. The Infantry past our camp on route for Medician Bow and this was the last of them.[44]

Tuesday 2nd 1877

Broke camp and made 20 mils and camped on North Plot River with plenty of wood in camp.

Wendsday 3rd 1877

Broke camp and made 18 mils and camped on a fork of Plot River. Very cold.

Thirsday 4th 1877

Left camp earley and made 12 mils and camped right at Fort Lorme [Laramie]. A good menney goot drunk here to day and I shiped my pipe home from hear that I had carried in my inside pocket ever since the fite.

Friday 5th 1877

Lay over all day and brought some [illegible] stuff and had a good supper. The 5 cavelry now left us and went to Ft. Russel.[45]

43. Lt. Col. Dodge remained at Fort Fetterman one day longer than did Col. Mackenzie and the cavalrymen. On Dec. 31, however, he began his march to Fort Laramie. Fort Riley, Kans., was his final destination. Gen. Crook also left Fort Fetterman that morning. Concerning the end of one year and the beginning of another, Dodge commented: "The last day of the Centennial year. In view of all the election vows, of the hardships of a winter Campaign, and of my verging into my 50th year—I could moralize quite lively tonight but that I am sleepy and have given orders for a very early start tomorrow. Morality is a good thing in civilization, but worth nothing, means nothing here." Dodge diary, Dec. 31, 1876, Newberry Library.

44. Dodge remarked that he and the infantrymen caught up with the horsemen on Horseshoe Creek. Mackenzie had hurried on toward Chicago and the troops were under Captain Mauck's command. See Dodge diary, Jan. 1, 1877, Newberry Library.

45. Fort D. A. Russell, in Cheyenne, Wyo.

Saturday 6th 1877

Broke camp and left for our old home in Red Cloud [Agency].
This is the first time we were let [k]now where we were a going.
We goot to Raw hide after going threw rane and mud all day. I
had on a nuff close for two men and I was wet to the skin all over
and my Boots fool of wotter.

This day I saw two soldiers stand off and shoot six shots a peace
at each other and never tuched a hare. Then one mounted his
horse and lit out and never come back a gane. Both of them were
drunk.

Durring the nite the wind come up and Lord it did turn cold.
Every thing frose stiff—tents and all and some of the tents blod
down and so did mine a long with the rest.

With this rather comic scene invoking images of soldiers help-
lessly sprawled beneath folds of canvas, Earl Smith concludes his
chronicle of the Powder River Expedition. The last glimpse he
gives of himself is a far cry from the images of heroic cavalrymen
in Frederic Remington's canvasses, or the pages of Lieutenant
Bourke's prose, or the official proclamation of General Crook that
announced the expedition's close:

The Brigadier General Commanding announces the close of the
Powder River Expedition and avails himself of the opportunity to
thank the officers and men composing it for the ability, courage,
endurance and zeal exhibited by them during its progress. With
the mercury exhibiting such extreme degrees of cold as to make
life well nigh unbearable, even when surrounded by the comforts
of civilization, you have endured with uncomplaining fortitude, the
rigors of the weather from which you had less to protect you than
an Indian is usually provided with.

The disintegration of many of the hostile bands of savages
against whom you have been operating, attests the success of the
brilliant fight made by the Cavalry with the Cheyennes on the
North Fork and your toilsome marches along the Powder River
and the Belle Fourche.

The uniform good conduct of the command has rendered it
difficult to distinguish one above the other.

It is a matter of solemn regret that you have to mourn the loss
of the distinguished and brilliant young Cavalry officer, First Lieutenant John A. McKinney, 4th Cavalry and the gallant enlisted
men who fell with him in the lonely gorges of the Big Horn Moun-

tains. May the fostering care, by a grateful country, of those who are personal sufferers in their deaths, prove that Republics are not ungrateful.[46]

Whether or not Earl Smith read (or heard) this statement is uncertain. He probably would have enjoyed it, for many young men want to cut a heroic figure in the eyes of others and many people want to believe their actions are significant and useful. Nevertheless, that final image of Smith struggling with his "blowed down" tent—in fact, the entire diary—belies heroism, at least as defined by Crook and others who have transported the history of the Indian Wars and the army that fought them from the realm of reality to that of romance.

Smith was not a romantic hero. He was simply human. Sometimes he displayed compassion toward others; sometimes he displayed fits of temper. Sometimes he endured the hardships without complaint; sometimes he growled. Always, he was an ordinary soldier—one of hundreds—who pondered neither the army's purpose nor that of the Northern Cheyennes, for Smith did not ruminate on the moral dimensions of the war. Nor, apparently, did the others—officers, enlisted men, scouts. He just followed orders and "tride to do right as near as [he] node how." Most of the others would have said the same.

Private William Earl Smith's viewpoint was most certainly limited. Again, the same could be said of everyone else's. Understanding the needs, concerns, and values of others is difficult— whether they are on the other side of a battlefield or the other side of an army tent. Yet Smith's vision, with all its limitations, adds an element of understanding and levity to the story of the Powder River Expedition and the war against the Northern Cheyenne people that official reports or officers' accounts alone can never provide. His voice, in the company of others, helps define the human dimensions of the past and makes an enduring point: all voices must be heard—those of the illustrious and the obscure, the Indian ally and the Indian enemy, the officer and the enlisted man—if this story is ever to transcend the ethnocentric and romantic in order to approximate the real.

46. General Order No. 10, Jan. 8, 1877, copy contained in Powder River Expedition Order Book, John G. Bourke Papers, USMA.

Epilogue

Not surprisingly, the army officers who participated in the Powder River Expedition of 1876 emphasized its positive results in their official and public statements. Lieutenant John Bourke, for example, claimed that the fight on the Red Fork broke the power of the Northern Cheyennes and led to their eventual surrender the following spring. But not all Bourke's contemporaries hailed the expedition as a success. General William T. Sherman, for one, pointed out a number of problems with the effort, including Crook's failure to provide sufficient food and forage for soldiers and animals. And, as already shown, Colonel Richard Dodge found much fault with Crook's methods, although he kept his criticisms private.[1]

Historians, too, have debated the significance of Colonel Ranald Mackenzie's attack on Dull Knife's village. On the one hand, destruction of the camp and capture of many Cheyenne horses certainly weakened the Northern Cheyennes' ability to resist the army. On the other hand, some argue, the victory was more an elaborate skirmish with negligible effects than a decisive battle

1. William Sherman to Philip Sheridan, Feb. 2, 1877, Special File, Sioux War 1876, Box 17, RG 393, Division of the Missouri, NARS; Dodge diary, Dec. 7 and 8, 1876, Newberry Library. See also a lengthy assessment of the entire campaign which concludes the Dodge diary. Bourke's view can be found in Bourke, *Mackenzie's Last*, 55.

that led to the downfall of the Cheyennes. Perhaps the most balanced view presents Mackenzie's attack as one of several that sapped the Indians' strength—a major disaster in a series of setbacks—leading to, but not solely responsible for, eventual surrender.[2]

The Cheyenne warrior Wooden Leg—supporting the view that the Dull Knife Battle did not destroy his people's determination to resist reservation life—claimed that during the spring of 1877 almost all of the Northern Cheyennes were camped on the upper Little Bighorn, where they lived in comfortable lodges and were "in every way . . . living yet according to [their] customary habits." They did not bother any whites, nor did the whites bother them: "We felt we were on our own land. We had killed only such people as had come for driving us away from it. So, our hearts were clean from any feeling of guilt."[3] Wooden Leg thus presented an image of the Northern Cheyennes as rebounding from the disaster on the Red Fork, rather than reeling into their ultimate collapse.

Even if Wooden Leg overstated the Cheyennes' recovery, it is certainly clear that Mackenzie's attack did not force an immediate surrender. After joining Crazy Horse's Oglalas in January, the Cheyennes gradually rebuilt their supplies of meat and hides for lodges. The difficulty of sustaining such a large group of people in the dead of winter, however, led to the eventual separation of the Sioux and the Cheyennes on Hanging Woman Creek, although some Oglalas remained with the main body of Northern Cheyennes and some Cheyennes remained with the main body of Oglalas.

In the meantime, army officials attempted to lure the Indians into agencies with promises that they would not be punished for wiping out Custer's men the previous summer. They would, though, be compelled to give up their firearms and their horses. Some Sioux and Cheyennes were seriously considering these terms when they received word that soldiers had captured several Cheyenne women and children, including Sweet Taste Woman, who had been traveling from the Oglala village to the Cheyenne

2. Nohl, "Mackenzie Against Dull Knife," 91–92.
3. Marquis, *Wooden Leg*, 294.

camp. While Colonel Nelson Miles held the captives at the army cantonment on the Tongue, some Cheyenne men attempted to rescue them but did not succeed.[4]

In early February 1877, Sweet Taste Woman arrived in the Cheyenne village with a message from Miles. If they surrendered peacefully, Miles would not punish them. She also reported the troopers treated the women and children captives well. Sweet Taste Woman then distributed sugar, flour, bacon, hardtack, and tobacco—gifts from the army officer. Members of the Council of Forty-four, as well as the chiefs of the military societies, deliberated Miles' offer. Some believed Miles was sincere. Others feared a trap: that after they surrendered their guns, the soldiers would kill them. Consequently, council members could not reach a consensus about surrender.[5]

Finally, Two Moon led a group into the Tongue River Cantonment and surrendered to Miles.[6] Within a few days, thirty of these Cheyenne men enlisted as scouts for the United States Army.[7] The majority, however, which included Morning Star, Little Wolf, and the other two Old Man Chiefs, elected to move east, spending the remainder of the winter with Crazy Horse's village on the Powder River. While encamped there, runners from Miles informed them of kind treatment at Fort Keogh. Seven Cheyennes from Red Cloud Agency also urged them to surrender there, with the renewed promise that they would not be punished. Once again, the chiefs gathered, but could not agree on a course of action. In the end, they decided each individual should choose for him or herself.[8]

On April 21, 1877, the four Old Man Chiefs—Morning Star, Little Wolf, Dirty Moccasins, and Old Bear—turned them-

4. Grinnell, *Fighting Cheyennes*, 383; Powell, *Sweet Medicine* 1:175–177; Stands in Timber, *Cheyenne Memories*, 222; Powell, *People* 2:1074–1078. Sweet Taste Woman was in her fifties and the widow of Black White Man, a black man the Cheyennes had captured many years before. Crooked Nose, sister of Wooden Leg, was among those women captured by troopers.

5. Grinnell, *Fighting Cheyennes*, 383–87; Powell, *Sweet Medicine* 1:184.

6. Others who surrendered with Two Moon included Crazy Head, White Wolf, White Hawk, Medicine Bear, White Elk, Howling Wolf, and Old Wolf or Cut Foot. See Stands in Timber, *Cheyenne Memories*, 223.

7. Grinnell, *Fighting Cheyennes*, 387.

8. Powell, *Sweet Medicine* 1:190–91.

selves in at Red Cloud Agency. With them came 254 people. Smaller bands continued to come in until May 15, by which time 869 Northern Cheyennes were living at the agency. Almost immediately, agents and army officers began pressing them to move to Indian Territory and join the Southern Cheyennes. General George Crook offered them three choices: (1) move to Indian Territory, (2) move to the Shoshone and Arapahoe Agency at Fort Washakie, or (3) remain at Camp Robinson for one year, after which authorities would decide their fate. The majority chose the last option. Yet, in council with Crook, their spokesman, Standing Elk—to the astonishment of the Cheyennes—announced that his people would move south. May 28, 1877, Lieutenant Henry W. Lawton and soldiers of the Fourth Cavalry led the Northern Cheyennes out of Camp Robinson and on their way to exile on the southern plains.[9]

From the outset, things went wrong in Indian Territory. Ague and fever struck these northern plainsmen. Insufficient buffalo and other game meant starving times, as well. On September 8, 1878, after a year of depression and desperation, Morning Star and Little Wolf led nearly three hundred men, women, and children out of exile and toward their former home along the Powder and Tongue rivers. With soldiers in pursuit, the leaders decided to split up. Little Wolf successfully evaded the army through the winter and eventually surrendered to Lieutenant W. P. Clark, the following March.[10]

Morning Star's group, however, was not as fortunate. Army troops apprehended them and brought them to Fort Robinson, where the commanding officer informed them they would have to return to Indian Territory. These Northern Cheyennes said they would not go. Finally, in January, the officer cut off their food in an attempt to increase the pressure on them to return south. In addition, he incarcerated Morning Star's one hundred and fifty people in an icy cold barracks, with no heat. After four days without food, still determined never to return south, the Cheyennes broke out of the barracks and attempted to flee— literally for their lives, for only sixty to seventy of the prisoners were fighting men and few carried firearms to defend themselves.

    9. Ibid., 196–97.
    10. Grinnell, *Fighting Cheyennes*, 398; Powell, *Sweet Medicine* 1:198–214.

"Through the Smoke Sprang the Daring Young Soldier"—Frederic Remington's 1897 oil painting of an incident during the January 1879 pursuit of Morning Star's Northern Cheyennes. Amon Carter Museum, Fort Worth.

In the melee, soldiers killed sixty-four Northern Cheyennes. Eight to ten others were never found. Of the survivors, twenty were shipped back to Indian Territory, and twenty-five were sent to the Sioux agency at Pine Ridge. Morning Star was one survivor who found his way to that agency after secreting himself and his family from soldiers for ten miserable days and then wandering in the direction of the agency for another eighteen.[11]

In the wake of this tragedy, public sentiment swayed in favor of the obviously determined Northern Cheyennes, although it was not until 1884 that President Chester Arthur created a small reservation on the Rosebud Creek for them. At last the federal gov-

11. Grinnell, *Fighting Cheyennes*, 426–27; Powell, *Sweet Medicine*, 215–77. For a lengthy report on this tragic episode see "Proceedings of a Board of Officers, Convened by Order of the Following Special Orders No. 8, Headquarters, Department of the Platte." Copy loaned to author from Fort Robinson Museum, Nebr.

ernment recognized their claim to that beloved north country. Little Wolf lived on the Rosebud for nearly thirty more years. Morning Star too lived out the remainder of his days in southeastern Montana, where he died around 1883. He was buried on a high butte near the valley of the Rosebud.[12] In the end, although at a terrible cost to so many of their people, the Northern Cheyennes had won their right to stay in the north. Many of their descendants continue to live there today.

And what of those who fought so hard to remove the Northern Cheyennes from this corner of the West? Ironically, none of the men featured here returned to the Powder River country. Ironically, the days ahead for Private Earl Smith, Colonel Ranald Mackenzie, and Sergeant Major Stephen Walsh carried their own tragedies, their own pain.

The sergeant major's difficulties began soon after the close of the campaign while the Fourth Cavalry was en route from Camp Robinson to its next station, Fort Sill, Indian Territory. On June 1, 1877, Smith's nemesis was reduced in rank from sergeant major to private by the sentence of garrison court-martial.[13] Unfortunately, no record of his offense can be found. During the rest of his military career, Walsh would never again achieve the post of sergeant major. On January 3, 1885, the old war horse, after giving nearly twenty years of his life to the United States Army, was discharged at Fort Lowell, Arizona Territory. Walsh, who was fifty-one years old and suffering from "old age and aublyopia," claimed he did not care to enter an old soldier's home. Ten days later, the used-up soldier married Hannah Eisenstine in Central City, New Mexico, and a little over one month later, he died from an overdose of opium.[14]

12. Grinnell, *Fighting Cheyennes*, 426–27.

13. According to the muster roll, Walsh was reduced from sergeant major to private by sentence of Garrison Court Martial, General Order No. 2, Headquarters, Cavalry Battalion, near Sidney, Nebr., June 1, 1877, en route from Camp Robinson, Nebr., to Fort Sill, Indian Territory. See April 30–June 30, 1877, Muster Roll, Field Staff & Band, 4th Cavalry, Box 958, RG 94, Records of the Adjutant General's Office, NARS. Unfortunately, no record of that court-martial remains to indicate the nature of Walsh's offense. On July 9, 1877, he was transferred from the Field Staff and Band to Company L, 4th Cavalry.

14. See Stephen Walsh Pension File, #375 129, RG 15, Records of the Veterans Administration, NARS. First Lt. E. R. Morris, assistant surgeon at nearby

The sordid details of Walsh's last days might have gone unrecorded had his bride not claimed the soldier's pension. The Bureau of Pensions, ever vigilant against potential fraud, launched an investigation into Hannah Walsh's character and uncovered details about the final days of the "grate" Sergeant Major. Mrs. Walsh testified that she first met the soldier at Fort Concho, Texas, in 1872 when she worked as a laundress for the army. By that time Hannah claimed she was already a widow, twice over. Around 1882, Walsh and Hannah became engaged, but she refused to marry him while he was in the army. During the betrothal they wrote "friendship letters" to one another, but never had "carnal relations." Nor, she insisted, had she ever had such relations with any men other than her husbands.

After his discharge, the couple married and took up housekeeping in her home. Mrs. Walsh later insisted that Stephen was sober when they wed, although he did drink "considerable" after. "I cannot say that he kept comparatively sober . . . he was a man that could stand lots of liquor. He had been on a little spree just before he died, but was never off of his feet." On the morning of February 15, while the couple lay in their bed, Mrs. Walsh heard her husband give three of the "terriblest" groans and then he died. An army doctor from nearby Fort Bayard came to the house, determined Walsh had died of an overdose of opium, and, according to the widow, removed the Sergeant Major's brains.[15]

Pension Bureau employees eventually questioned a number of surgeons and officers at Fort Bayard about Walsh's death. Lieutenant W. H. Carter, of the Sixth Cavalry, presented a rather different view of the old soldier's final days. Carter's forage master had known Walsh for twenty years and reported several times that Walsh was "on a protracted drunk with an old whore who had followed up the 4th Cavalry for many years (from Texas). I only know the woman by sight," Carter explained, "and by unsavory reputation." He continued:

Fort Bayard, N. Mex., conducted the post-mortem examination and concluded Walsh died of opium poisoning. Other documents in the pension file attribute his death to apoplexy and rheumatic disorder of brain and heart and loss of sight.

15. Ibid.

In my opinion Walsh did not know what he was doing when he married the woman. He was drunk, and from his character when sober, I am sure he would scorn the idea of this woman's drawing a pension as his wife. My opinion formed at the time was that Walsh was disgusted at himself for his conduct and committed suicide. I believe I had his coffin made, and gave permission to the men under me to attend his funeral, more because I thought he had been unfortunate in getting in such a mess than anything else. Certainly I say the Government would do a criminal act to allow a pension to such a woman for such a marriage.[16]

Hannah Walsh's reputation, far more than Stephen Walsh's, determined the Board of Pension's decision with respect to her claim as widow. When it came to such matters, she did have her defenders, though they were half-hearted at best. John C. Givens, the United States commissioner of central New Mexico, who married the Walshes, testified that Walsh was sober at the wedding and the bride "was not a woman of the town, nor a sporting woman exactly." One special examiner, who found her visiting a respectable family in Henley, Texas, decided she was "not quite so 'black' perhaps as she had been painted. I found her a quiet, mild-mannered gray haired old lady. . . . While she was following the 4th Cav. from post to post, doing laundry work & c. it is very probable that she walked not strictly in virtue's path, but that she was an out and out prostitute, I do not think."[17]

Another special examiner, however, judged differently. To him "she was more man than woman." Moreover, he found her statement that she had carnal knowledge of no men besides her husbands preposterous and offered as proof a doctor's testimony that "there was *no doubt* but that she had at sometime been treated for 'syphilitic iritis.' " On June 27, 1893, Hannah Walsh's claim for the sergeant major's pension was denied and the case closed.[18]

Drunkenness, venereal disease, insanity, and scandal also char-

16. Lt. Carter penned this opinion March 28, 1889. See Stephen Walsh Pension File #375 129, RG 15, NARS.

17. John C. Givens' statement was dated Dec. 19, 1892. George M. Flick, Special Examiner, to Commissioner of Pensions, April 25, 1893, Stephen Walsh Pension File, #375 129, RG 15, NARS.

18. O. W. Lee, Special Examiner, to Commissioner of Pensions, Oct. 10, 1892, Stephen Walsh Pension File, #375 129, RG 15, NARS.

acterized Colonel Ranald Mackenzie's last days with the United States Army. From the end of the Powder River Expedition and the beginning of Mackenzie's tenure at Fort Sill, Indian Territory, according to one biographer, "Mackenzie grew more and more sensitive. He began to complain frequently of real or imagined ills. His tendency to feel persecuted (if not martyred) stood out in ever-bolder relief, until the colonel embarked on the dark trail of insanity."[19]

For the next six years, however, Mackenzie continued to carry out his duties on the southern plains. In May 1878 he led eleven companies of cavalrymen across the Rio Grande in pursuit of Kickapoos and cattle thieves. He did not catch them, but did attract the Mexican Army, with whom he had a brush. That summer he again crossed the international boundary, but he was called back by officials in Washington. In other military matters after the Dull Knife fight, Mackenzie served at Fort Garland, Colorado, and in the Military District of Arkansas, Arizona, and then Santa Fe, New Mexico, where in 1881 he was appointed brigadier general. Finally, in November 1883, General Mackenzie received command of the Department of Texas.

From all appearances things went well for him. Professionally he was a success. And Mackenzie's personal life held promise as well. Although he had never married, the increasingly frail and nervous general was reunited with a love of younger days, Florida Tunstall, when he took up residence at Fort Sam Houston. Circumstances had interfered with his romance years before and in 1864 the young woman had married an army doctor, Redford Sharpe. Now, in 1883, Mackenzie had another chance, for she was a widow. They became engaged, but never wed, for Mackenzie's final mental breakdown, characterized by erratic actions, public drunkenness, disorderly conduct, and even violent behavior, canceled not only his marriage plans but his military career as well.[20]

The end came fast. On December 19, 1883, officials from the Department of Texas telegraphed the Adjutant General's Office in Washington, D.C., that General Mackenzie was "suffering from mental aberration and [was] not able to exercise command."

19. Nohl, "Mackenzie Against Dull Knife," 159.
20. Wallace, "General Ranald Slidell Mackenzie," 392–96.

Working in concert with the general's sister, Harriet, the officer's colleagues spirited him out of Texas on a special car tendered by the Missouri Pacific Railroad. On December 29, Mackenzie was admitted to the Bloomingdale Asylum in New York. He was diagnosed as suffering from "general paresis." The illness, according to his doctors, could be attributed to a fall from a wagon at Fort Sill in 1875, as well as to a bout of sunstroke that he had as a child. But his diagnosis came, according to one of Mackenzie's biographers, three decades before the medical world realized that a "very high percentage" of these cases originated in syphilitic infection. "As unlikely as it may seem that the strait-laced general contracted syphilis," this historian writes, "the evidence strongly suggests that such was the case." Mackenzie exhibited nearly all the classic symptoms—irritability, restlessness, poor emotional control, and delusions of grandeur and persecution.[21]

The next March, a United States Army Retiring Board convened at the asylum to consider the case of Ranald Mackenzie. In the presence of the illustrious military hero, several doctors testified to his insanity and their inability to cure it. At this point, the general was allowed to plead his own case. In a calm, lucid manner he said, "I think that I am not insane. I think that I have served as faithfully as anybody in the army. I would rather die than go on the retired list. The army is all I have got to care for. I don't wish to stay here."

After one more doctor certified that Mackenzie suffered from "general paralysis of the insane" and was not likely to recover, the general presented the last word: "You all know me, and have known me a great many years. And I think it very harsh if I am left out of the army where my services have always been gallant and honest and faithful. And for a few months sickness. I think it will be very hard if I am separated from the active list of the army." This rather pathetic plea no doubt touched the hearts of the officers who heard it. Yet, they ultimately concluded, he was incapacitated for active service, discreetly indicating in the official record that his disability "was incurred from wounds received and exposure in the line of duty."[22]

21. Ranald S. Mackenzie Military Service Record, #3877 ACP 1873, Box 202, RG 94, NARS; Nohl, "Bad Hand," 328–29.

22. Ranald S. Mackenzie Military Service Record, #3877 ACP 1873, Box 202, RG 94.

In June the Bloomingdale Asylum discharged Ranald Mackenzie, who took up residence with his sister in Morristown, New
Jersey. A few letters from his increasingly unsteady hand remain
among his military service records as documentation of both his
deteriorating health and his pitiful hope that he would soon recover and regain his position in the army. On January 19, 1889,
General Mackenzie died on Staten Island, New York, a long distance from the Red Fork of the Powder River. He was only forty-
eight years old.[23]

One can only wonder if William Earl Smith ever learned of his
former "Genrall's" death and only speculate what he might have
thought of such an end. By 1889, Smith was back in Illinois and,
once again, working as a railroadman. His own separation from
the army had been equally traumatic and painful, although under
different circumstances. Moreover, there would be in his own
death, which did not come until 1909, a final and haunting link
to Ranald Mackenzie.

Private Smith's army days lasted until October 3, 1878, when
he "took [his] bundle and left," two and one-half years into his
original five-year enlistment.[24] By the fall of 1878 he could no
longer abide army life and so he deserted. The urge to leave grew
gradually after the Powder River Expedition's close. Smith and the
Fourth Cavalry had left Camp Robinson on May 28, 1877,
marching to Fort Wallace, Kansas, where they remained until
December, passing the time in regular post and escort duty.[25]

During that summer Smith's mother, now Mrs. William H.
Thompson of Rock Island, Illinois, began efforts to free her son
from his military obligation, presumably at his request. In a June
1877 letter to the secretary of war, Mrs. Thompson asked for an
honorable discharge. "I feel as though I should have him at
home—he is subject," she explained, "to cholera and as he is my
oldest, I am very much attached to him. My own health is failing
having hemorages from the lungs. I feel as though I should not

23. Ibid.
24. William Earl Smith diary, Oct. 3, 1878, typescript copy owned by author. Charles Smith, Crystal Lake, Ill., owns the original diary. See also Aug.
31–Oct. 31, 1876, Muster Roll, Box 968, Company E, 4th Cavalry, RG 94,
NARS.
25. See various muster rolls, 1877–1878, Company E, 4th Cavalry, Box 968,
RG 94, NARS.

see him again should he stay much longer. . . . Please give attention to the above and relieve a mother's mind."[26] Her pleas, however, went unheeded.

On January 1, 1878, Smith picked up his pencil and began
keeping a journal once again. "A happy New Year," he wrote.
"The long looked for day has come and finds me out in the West
at Fort Sill, I.T. and on gard as Ordley Trumpter and can blow
till my hart is contented for that is all a man can do that is in the
same fix as I am in."[27] Not long after, Earl and the others marched
to Fort Duncan, Texas, via Forts Richardson, Mason, and Clark,
arriving February 25.[28] While encamped at Fort Richardson,
which he pronounced "a hard looking post and town," Smith was
promoted to corporal. "It sounds funey to me," he conceded to
his diary. "Some of the boys dont like it much, I gess, and I dont
care a dam. This world is but a buble and nothing hear but
woe."[29]

The following months brought mostly frontier-duty drudgery,
which Corporal Smith broke up by borrowing an occasional book
from the library, writing letters home, playing billiards with the
boys, and shooting jack rabbits. A riding accident undermined his
morale. In April while he was pursuing a band of Mexican raiders
along the Rio Grande, Smith's horse bucked him off and he in-
jured his back.[30] From that point on he complained of back aches
and illness. In August and September he spent over three weeks
in the hospital.

26. Mrs. William H. Thompson to George W. McCrary, June 9, 1877, RG
94, Enlisted Branch, Letters Received, NARS. She wrote similar letters to the
Secretary of War, Oct. 3, 1877, and to Mr. Henderson, Nov. 18, 1877. Her final
appeal, in an undated (1878) letter to G. W. McCrary, reached her son's post
only after he had deserted. See Box 2289, RG 94, Enlisted Branch, Letters
Received, NARS.

27. William Earl Smith diary, Jan. 1, 1878, typescript in author's possession.

28. Dec. 31, 1877–Feb. 28, 1878, Muster Roll, Company E, 4th Cavalry,
Box 968, RG 94, NARS.

29. William Earl Smith diary, Jan. 25 and 26, 1878, typescript in author's
possession. A corporal was paid $15 per month, and so this promotion meant
an increase in Smith's pay. Coffman, Old Army, 347.

30. Smith diary, April 4, 1878; see also Feb. 28, 1878–April 30, 1878, Muster Roll, Company E, 4th Cavalry, Box 968, RG 94, NARS; and William Earl
Smith medical records, Carded Medical Records, 4th U.S. Cavalry, RG 94, Records of the Adjutant General's Office, NARS.

To make matters worse, his physical ailments took their toll on his temperament. On August 18, 1878, a prisoner struck Corporal Smith, while the latter was putting him under guard. Smith responded by breaking "a carbine over his hed."[31] One month later the corporal was again put in charge of some prisoners and again, as he put it, "got off of [his] eggs." This time he was arrested and placed under guard. "They aire a going to hook me up now for what good I have done."[32] Just exactly what Smith *did* do is uncertain since the record of the ensuing court-martial cannot be found. Nevertheless, on October 1, Corporal Smith was tried. Although he pled not guilty, the court found him otherwise. His sentence reduced him to the rank of private and fined him ten dollars.[33] Two days later, with his sergeant refusing to excuse him from any duty, and still in pain, Smith deserted. He spent his first night on the lam in a haystack and "got good and drunk over it."[34] Ironically, unbeknown to Smith, the court-martial decision had been overturned by a higher authority, on the basis of a technicality.[35] Had Smith remained at his post, his rank of corporal would have been reinstated. Instead, he had skipped and now faced much more serious consequences, should authorities apprehend him, or should he choose to surrender.

In deserting from the frontier army, Smith selected an option that appealed to many other soldiers of the period. According to War Department counts, one-third of the men recruited between 1867 and 1891 had deserted. Furthermore, desertion did not

31. Smith diary, Aug. 18, 1878.

32. Ibid., Sept. 19, 1878.

33. Ibid., Oct. 1, 1878. Unfortunately, no record of this court-martial survives at NARS.

34. Ibid., Oct. 3, 1878.

35. 1st Endorsement, Judge Advocate's Office, San Antonio, Texas, Oct. 7, 1878, Garrison Court-Martial File 704, RG 153, Records of the Judge Advocate General's Office, NARS. The endorsement reads: "Respectfully returned with the recommendation that this case be returned to the Commanding Office Camp near Strickland Springs, Tex. for revocation of his approval of the proceedings, findings and sentence for the reason that the record shows affirmatively that the Court commenced its sessions after 3 P.M. and sets forth no authority therefore from the officer appointing the Court.

"Moreover, the Department Commander has frequently expressed his disapproval of trials of non-commissioned officers for breach of arrest, and has directed that his decision thereon below quoted shall govern in his Department."

carry the stigma in the late nineteenth century that it would in the twentieth. It was not, according to one historian, "considered an especially dastardly offense, and many civilians in the West sympathized with deserters."[36] Even some army officers empathized with them. William Paulding, who served as an officer at Fort Clark, Texas, around the time Smith deserted, later recalled a detail where he pursued some deserters, shackled them, and brought them back to the post:

> I felt sorry for one of them as he was only a boy, and evidently had been led off by the others, but there was nothing that could be done for him as he had deserted. I do not remember what his sentence was, but most likely a dishonorable discharge with loss of all pay and from two to five years in prison as that was the average sentence. When one comes to think of the life a soldier led in those days, no amusements or pleasures, uncomfortable beds & none to [sic] good food in some companies . . . one cannot help but feel sorry for them, not all however, but the young fellows who no doubt were homesick and did not realize what they were doing until too late.[37]

Enlisted men's reasons for deserting varied, of course. But most often men left because of harsh treatment by officers, economic inducements outside the army (in railroading or mining, for example), or loneliness. Some, fearing an upcoming court-martial, preferred desertion to facing the consequences of their transgressions.[38] Private Smith apparently left for a number of reasons that included his illnesses and injuries, his anger over his own recent court-martial and reduction in rank, and a general dissatisfaction with army life.

The army did not conduct extensive searches for deserters and, consequently, the majority of them were never caught. In the last third of the nineteenth century, those who were retrieved and tried usually served out the unexpired balance of their original

36. Don Rickey, Jr., *Forty Miles*, 143. See also Coffman, *The Old Army*, 371–79.

37. William Paulding, unpublished reminiscence, William Paulding Papers, U.S. Military History Institute, Carlisle Barracks, Pa.

38. See Jack Foner, "The United States Soldier Between Two Wars: Army Life and Reforms, 1865–1898" (Ph.D. diss., Columbia University, 1968), 24–25; Rickey, *Forty Miles*, 152–53.

enlistments, or else their remaining enlistment time was added onto a prison sentence. The average prison sentence came to about two years of hard labor, although sometimes the sentence was reduced by one year or increased to three or four years. In addition, prisoners frequently found themselves restrained by ball and chain during the course of their sentence. By 1873 so many regulars had deserted, however, that general amnesty was declared. Officials offered deserters the option to surrender in exchange for returning to normal duty. Their only punishment would be serving, in addition to their regular enlistment period, the time lost while absent without leave.[39]

Earl Smith must have hoped such leniency would prevail when he surrendered in Chicago on March 4, 1879. A general court-martial convened April 2 at Jefferson Barracks, Missouri, to hear his case, and Smith answered guilty to the charge of desertion. The judge advocate then read to the court Smith's statement of defense:

> I William E. Smith, Co. E, 4th Cavalry did desert my company at Fort Clark, Texas on the 4th day of October, 1878, and I do affirm that the reason which actuated me in so doing was the pain I suffered doing duty in consequence of being thrown from my horse about three months before my desertion. From the effects of that accident I have not yet fully recovered, and I am afraid that I never again will be able to ride in the saddle without enduring serious pain.
>
> I enlisted in the service of the United States on the 2nd day of February 1876 and joined my company on the 28th day of March 1876. I was a private for eighteen months after I enlisted and served as orderly for General Mackenzie during the Sioux campaign of 1876. After our return from the campaign, I was made trumpeter which duty I did until I was made a non-commissioned officer by orders of Captain [D. A.] Irwin, and which position I held until within two days of my desertion.
>
> It seemed almost compulsory on me to desert as I was suffering severely from the fall, to which I have alluded above. During the time I served in the Army I used my best endeavors to do my duty acceptably to my superior officer and during that time was in the guard house but once. I never had thought of deserting my company until about two hours before doing so and then should not

39. Rickey, *Forty Miles*, 152–53.

have done so, had I not known or believed that I would not be able
to do my duty as a soldier.[40]

When I deserted, I took nothing with me belonging to the government, or to my superior officers, or my commander, not even
taking what was virtually my own as I had One hundred and forty
five dollars in the hands of the U.S. Paymaster, besides which I
had saved over fifty dollars in clothing money and all of which was
necessarily lost to me. I was afraid to go home after deserting and
went west as far as Sacramento where I secured employment on
the Central Pacific R.R. Here though the thought of what I had
done and the fear of arrest drove me to throw up my employment.
My friends were constantly imploring me to come home and these
solicitations added to my feeling of arrest, induced me at last to go
home where I speedily secured employment on the C.B. & Q. R.R.
[Chicago, Burlington and Quincy Railroad]. Even at home though,
the feeling that I was a deserter constantly haunted me day and
night giving me no peace of mind whatever. The keen sorrow
which my poor mother would feel to see me dragged from home
as a deserter, rendered my life unbearable, so that at last I sought
advise [sic] from my friends as to what I should better do, and this
advise agreeing with my own opinion, I finally gave up my job and
started for Chicago, upon my arrival at which city I surrendered
myself to the proper authorities. I have nothing further to state,
but sincerely hope that you will carefully consider the circumstances to which I allude, and further hoping that your delibera-
tions may be tempered with feeling of mercy I leave my case in
your hands.[41]

The members of the court that day, however, did not feel particularly merciful. They found him guilty and sentenced him to a
dishonorable discharge and a three-year prison term.[42] On May 8,

40. His diary indicates Smith thought about deserting at least one week before he actually did so. On Sept. 26 he wrote, "Thought I would take a skip at
nite but gave it up for the other fellow did not want to walk." And on Sept. 29
he considered desertion again: "Not much to day only I think I and the Army
will stop to nite. But changed my mind and will stay on." William Earl Smith
diary, Sept. 26 and 28, 1878, typescript in author's possession.

41. Smith's defense statement was dated March 16, 1879. Court-Martial
Case File QQ 1073, Box 1906, RG 153, Records of the Office of the Judge
Advocate General (Army), NARS.

42. Ibid. The officers detailed for Smith's court-martial included Surgeon E.
P. Valluin; Maj. J. F. Wade, Ninth Cavalry; Capt. J. H. Gageby, 3d Infantry; Lt.
F. M. Gibson, 7th Cavalry; Lt. Charles Morton, 3d Cavalry; and Lt. C. H.
Rockwell, 5th Cavalry.

With army life behind him, Smith returned to Peoria, where he married soon after this portrait was taken. Credit: Charles Watts

1879, Fort Leavenworth Prison received Earl Smith. Perhaps the news, several months later, that his sentence was reduced to two years helped him through those difficult days. Throughout his stay in prison, Smith's mother pleaded with her congressman, the secretary of war, and anyone else she thought might help, to release her son. Finally, on December 24, 1880, Earl walked out of Fort Leavenworth's prison gate and forever ended his relationship with the United States Army.[43]

43. See William E. Smith, Register of Prisoners at U.S. Military Prison at Fort Leavenworth, RG 393, Records of the U.S. Army Continental Commands, 1821–1920, NARS. The order promulgating Smith's sentence was dated April 25, 1879, and he entered Fort Leavenworth Prison on May 8, 1879. His occupation was listed as teamster. Although his original term was to expire April 24, 1882, his sentence was reduced by one year, by order of Gen. William Sherman.

By June 1882 Smith had returned to Peoria to wed Anna E. Murphy and resumed his old line of work, railroading.[44] In 1883 their first child, a daughter named Jennie, in honor of Earl's sister, was born. In the next eight years Earl and Anna had children at two-year intervals, three sons named Foster, Royal, and Charles, and another daughter, named Carrie.

The sagebrush soldier's last days were not peaceful ones, however. At the age of fifty-seven, he died in Chicago of "general paresis of the insane," the same, sad malady that struck down Ranald Mackenzie twenty years before.[45] One other time, on an icy winter morning along the banks of the Red Fork in the Big

---

See Court-Martial Case File QQ 1073, Special Orders No. 157, July 7, 1879, Headquarters of the Army, Adjutant General's Office, RG 153, Box 1906, NARS. Smith was discharged Dec. 24, 1880. After succeeding in reducing her son's sentence by 1 year, Mrs. Thompson appealed for an additional 6 months' reprieve. In the appeal she offered the following: "Several have been discharged that went at the same time for the same offence. I get letters from my son every month begging me to do something for him. My health is very bad, constant woring [sic] is breaking me down. My son has had good character from Gen. McKensie (whom he was with at the Black Hills) and from his Captain Irwin. . . . Excuse this badly written letter as I am most too weak to hold a pen." Mrs. William Thompson to Thomas J. Henderson, April 26, 1880, RG 94, Records of the Adjutant General's Office, Enlisted Branch, Letters Received, NARS.

This time, however, the Bureau of Military Justice did not respond favorably to her request: "The Prisoner's statement" (during the court-martial proceedings) "leaves it more than questionable whether he did not rather desert because of his reduction to the ranks than in consequence of bodily pain; of which he had been discharged cured from the hospital, and which did not interfere with his earning his support by labor on railroads. No public reason is seen to present itself for considering favorably Mrs. Thompson's petition." See Judge Advocate General to Secretary of War, May 5, 1880, RG 153, Records of the Judge Advocate General's Office, NARS.

44. William Earl Smith and Anna Murphy, Marriage License, June 1, 1882, Peoria County Courthouse, Peoria, Ill. According to the license, Smith was 29 and Murphy was 23.

45. According to the death certificate, a contributing cause of Smith's death was syphilis, which the attending doctor estimated he had had for about 20 years. He suffered from "general paresis of the insane" for about 3 years. At the time of his death, which occurred Oct. 25, 1909, Smith's occupation was listed as switchman. See Earl W. Smith, Death Certificate, Bureau of Vital Statistics, Department of Health, City of Chicago, Chicago, Illinois.

Horn Mountains, these two had shared in tragedy as they drank hot coffee and talked quietly about the terrible sacrifices war required. In their own deaths, far from that snowy battlefield, they came together again. The gap between officer and orderly closed one last time.

Bibliography

Manuscript Collections

Denver Public Library, Denver, Colorado
  John Gregory Bourke Diaries (microfilm copies).
National Archives (NARS), Washington, D.C.
  Record Group 15, Records of the Veterans Administration
  Record Group 94, Records of the Adjutant General's Office, 1780s–
    1917
  Record Group 153, Records of the Judge Advocate General's Office
  Record Group 393, Records of the United States Army Continental
    Commands, 1821–1920
Nebraska State Historical Society, Lincoln, Nebraska
  Eli Seavey Ricker Collection
Newberry Library, Chicago, Illinois
  Richard Irving Dodge Papers
  Henry Lawton Papers
  1850–Illinois–Peoria County–Peoria Federal Census (microfilm)
  1860–Illinois–Peoria County–Peoria Federal Census (microfilm)
  1870–Illinois–Peoria County–Peoria Federal Census (microfilm)
New York Public Library, New York, New York
  James S. McClellan Papers
United States Army Military History Institute, Carlisle Barracks,
    Pennsylvania

Order of the Indian Wars Collection
William Paulding Papers
United States Military Academy Library (USMA), West Point, New York
John G. Bourke Papers
Joseph H. Dorst Papers
Western Heritage Center, University of Wyoming, Laramie
"Indian-Battle–Dull Knife" file

Published Primary Sources, Including Newspapers

Bourke, Captain John G. *Mackenzie's Last Fight with the Cheyennes: A Winter Campaign in Wyoming and Montana.* New York: Argonaut Press, 1966.

Buecker, Thomas R., ed. "The Journals of James S. McClellan 1st Sgt., Company H. 3rd Cavalry." *Annals of Wyoming* 57 (Spring 1985): 21–34.

Carter, R. G. *On The Border With Mackenzie, or Winning West Texas From the Comanches.* New York: Antiquarian Press, 1961.

Cheyenne Daily Leader. See issues for August 8, August 11, October 25 and 31, November 18, 19, 21, 29, 30, December 2, 6, 1876.

Dodge, Richard Irving. *The Powder River Expedition Journals of Colonel Richard Irving Dodge.* Ed. Wayne R. Kime. Norman: University of Oklahoma Press, 1997.

Grant, Ulysses. *Personal Memoirs of U.S. Grant.* Vol. 1. New York: Charles L. Webster & Co., 1886.

Hedren, Paul L. "Campaigning with the 5th Cavalry: Private James B. Frew's Diary and Letters from the Great Sioux War of 1876." *Nebraska History* 65 (Winter 1984): 433–66.

King, Captain Charles. *Campaigning with Crook.* Norman: University of Oklahoma Press, 1964.

Marquis, Thomas B. *Wooden Leg: A Warrior Who Fought Custer.* Lincoln: University of Nebraska Press, 1931.

North, Luther. *Man of the Plains: Recollections of Luther North, 1856–1882.* Lincoln: University of Nebraska Press, 1961.

Schmitt, Martin F., ed. *General George Crook: His Autobiography.* Norman: University of Oklahoma Press, 1946.

"The Sioux War." *Harper's Weekly.* 20 (Dec. 16, 1876): 1018.

Stands in Timber, John, and Margot Liberty. *Cheyenne Memories.* Lincoln: University of Nebraska Press, 1972.

Unrau, William E., ed. *Tending the Talking Wire: A Buck Soldier's View of Indian Country, 1863–1866.* Salt Lake City: University of Utah Press, 1972.

Wheeler, Homer W. *The Frontier Trail, or from Cowboy to Colonel.* Los Angeles: Times-Mirror Press, 1923.

Secondary Sources

Berthrong, Donald J. *The Southern Cheyennes*. Norman: University of Oklahoma Press, 1963.

Brady, Cyrus Townsend. *Indian Fights and Fighters*. New York: Mc-Clure, Phillips & Co., 1904.

Brown, Mark H. *The Plainsmen of the Yellowstone*. New York: G. P. Putnam's Sons, 1961.

Buecker, Thomas R. and R. Eli Paul. "The Pawnee Scouts: Mounted Auxiliaries." *Military Images* 7 (July–Aug. 1985): 16–19.

Clow, Richmond L. "General Philip Sheridan's Legacy: The Sioux Pony Campaign of 1876." *Nebraska History* 57 (Winter 1976): 461–77.

Coffman, Edward M. *The Old Army: A Portrait of the American Army in Peacetime, 1784–1898*. New York: Oxford University Press, 1986.

Dunlay, Thomas W. *Wolves for the Blue Soldiers: Indian Scouts and Auxiliaries with the United States Army, 1860–1890*. Lincoln: University of Nebraska Press, 1982.

Easton, Karen. "Getting Into Uniform: Northern Cheyenne Scouts in the United States Army, 1876–81." Master's thesis, University of Wyoming, 1985.

Foner, Jack. "The United States Soldier Between Two Wars: Army Life and Reforms, 1865–1898." Ph.D. diss., Columbia University, 1968.

Frazer, Robert W. *Forts of the West: Military Forts and Presidios and Posts Commonly Called Forts West of the Mississippi River to 1898*. Norman: University of Oklahoma Press, 1965.

Grange, Roger T. "Fort Robinson, Outpost on the Plains." *Nebraska History* 39 (Sept. 1958): 191–240.

Gray, John S. *Centennial Campaign: The Sioux War of 1876*. Fort Collins, Colo.; Old Army Press, 1976. Reprint, Norman University of Oklahoma Press, 1988.

Greene, Jerome A. *Slim Buttes, 1876: An Episode of the Great Sioux War*. Norman: University of Oklahoma Press, 1982.

Grinnell, George Bird. *By Cheyenne Campfires*. Lincoln: University of Nebraska Press, 1971.

———. *The Cheyenne Indians: Their History and Ways of Life*. New York: Cooper Square Publishers, Inc., 1962.

———. *The Fighting Cheyennes*. Norman: University of Oklahoma Press, 1963.

Heitman, Francis B. *Historical Register and Dictionary of the United States Army*. Washington, D.C.: Government Printing Office, 1903.

Hoebel, E. Adamson. *The Cheyennes: Indians of the Great Plains.* New York: Holt, Rinehart and Winston, 1978.

Hutton, Paul Andrew. *Phil Sheridan and His Army.* Lincoln: University of Nebraska Press, 1985.

————, ed. *Soldiers West: Biographies from the Military Frontier.* Lincoln: University of Nebraska Press, 1987.

Hyde, George E. *Red Cloud's Folk: A History of the Oglala Sioux Indians.* Norman: University of Oklahoma Press, 1937.

————. *Spotted Tail's Folk: A History of the Brulé Sioux.* Norman: University of Oklahoma Press, 1961.

Keegan, John. *The Face of Battle.* New York: Viking Press, 1976.

Knight, Oliver. *Following the Indian Wars: The Story of the Newspaper Correspondents Among the Indian Campaigners.* Norman: University of Oklahoma Press, 1960.

Limerick, Patricia Nelson. *The Legacy of Conquest: The Unbroken Past of the American West.* New York: W. W. Norton & Co., 1987.

Mangum, Neil C. *Battle of the Rosebud: Prelude to the Little Bighorn.* El Segundo, Calif.: Upton & Sons, 1987.

Milner, Clyde A. *With Good Intentions: Quaker Work Among the Pawnees, Otos and Omahas in the 1870's.* Lincoln: University of Nebraska Press, 1982.

Murray, Robert A. *Military Posts in the Powder River Country of Wyoming, 1865–1894.* Lincoln: University of Nebraska Press, 1968.

————. *Military Posts of Wyoming.* Fort Collins, Colo.: Old Army Press, 1974.

Nohl, Lessing H. "Bad Hand: The Military Career of Ranald Slidell Mackenzie, 1871–1889." Ph.D. diss., University of New Mexico, 1962.

————. "Mackenzie Against Dull Knife: Breaking the Northern Cheyennes in 1876." In *Probing the American West: Papers from the Santa Fe Conference,* ed. K. Ross Toole et al. Santa Fe: Museum of New Mexico Press, 1962.

Olson, James C. *Red Cloud and the Sioux Problem.* Lincoln: University of Nebraska Press, 1965.

Pierce, Michael D. *The Most Promising Young Officer: A Life of Ranald Slidell Mackenzie.* Norman: University of Oklahoma Press, 1993.

Porter, Joseph C. *Paper Medicine Man: John Gregory Bourke and His American West.* Norman: University of Oklahoma Press, 1986.

Powell, Peter J. *People of the Sacred Mountain: A History of the Northern Cheyenne Chiefs and Warrior Societies, 1830–1879.* 2 vols. San Francisco: Harper & Row, 1981.

————. *Sweet Medicine: The Continuing Role of the Sacred Arrows, the Sun Dance, and the Sacred Buffalo Hat in Northern Cheyenne History.* Norman: University of Oklahoma Press, 1969.

Rickey, Don, Jr. *Forty Miles a Day on Beans and Hay.* Norman: University of Oklahoma Press, 1976.

Smith, Sherry L. "The Bozeman: Trail to Death and Glory." *Annals of Wyoming* 55 (Spring 1983): 32–50.

———. "'Civilization's Guardians': U.S. Army Officers' Reflections on Indians and the Indian Wars in the Trans-Mississippi West, 1848–1890." Ph.D. diss., University of Washington, 1984.

Utley, Robert M. *Frontier Regulars: The United States Army and the Indian, 1866–1890.* New York: Macmillan Publishing Co., 1973.

———. *The Indian Frontier of the American West, 1846–1890.* Albuquerque: University of New Mexico Press, 1984.

Wallace, Edward S. "General Ranald Slidell Mackenzie: Indian Fighting Cavalryman." *Southwestern Historical Quarterly* 56 (Jan. 1953): 378–96.

Werner, Fred H. *The Dull Knife Battle.* Greeley, Colo.: Werner Publications, 1981.

West, Elliott. *The Contested Plains: Indians, Goldseekers and the Road to Colorado.* Lawrence: University Press of Kansas, 1998.

White, Richard. "The Winning of the West: The Expansion of the Western Sioux in the Eighteenth and Nineteenth Centuries." *Journal of American History* 65 (Sept. 1978): 319–43.

Wooster, Robert. *The Military and United States Indian Policy, 1865–1903.* New Haven and London: Yale University Press, 1988.

Index